LETTERS OF NOTE: MOTHERS

Letters of Note was born in 2009 with the launch of lettersofnote.com, a website celebrating old-fashioned correspondence that has since been visited over 100 million times. The first *Letters of Note* volume was published in October 2013, followed later that year by the first Letters Live, an event at which world-class performers delivered remarkable letters to a live audience.

Since then, these two siblings have grown side by side, with *Letters of Note* becoming an international phenomenon, and Letters Live shows being staged at iconic venues around the world, from London's Royal Albert Hall to the theatre at the Ace Hotel in Los Angeles.

You can find out more at lettersofnote.com and letterslive.com. And now you can also listen to the audio editions of the new series of *Letters of Note*, read by an extraordinary cast drawn from the wealth of talent that regularly takes part in the acclaimed Letters Live shows.

Letters of Note

Mothers

COMPILED BY

Shaun Usher

PENGUIN BOOKS

For all mothers,
but especially my own

PENGUIN BOOKS
An imprint of Penguin Random House LLC
penguinrandomhouse.com

First published in Great Britain by Canongate Books Ltd 2020
Published in Penguin Books 2021

LIBRARY OF CONGRESS CATALOGING-IN-PUBLICATION DATA
Names: Usher, Shaun, 1978– editor.
Title: Letters of note. Mothers / Shaun Usher.
Other titles: Mothers
Description: New York : Penguin Books, 2021. | Series: Letters of note |
Identifiers: LCCN 2020027942 (print) | LCCN 2020027943 (ebook) |
ISBN 9780143134725 (paperback) | ISBN 9780525506539 (ebook)
Subjects: LCSH: Mothers—Correspondence. | Mother and child. |
Motherhood. | Letters.
Classification: LCC HQ759 .L4737 2021 (print) |
LCC HQ759 (ebook) | DDC 306.874/3—dc23
LC record available at https://lccn.loc.gov/2020027942
LC ebook record available at https://lccn.loc.gov/2020027943

Printed in the United States of America
1st Printing

Set in Joanna MT

CONTENTS

A letter is a time bomb, a message in a bottle, a spell, a cry for help, a story, an expression of concern, a ladle of love, a way to connect through words. This simple and brilliantly democratic art form remains a potent means of communication and, regardless of whatever technological revolution we are in the middle of, the letter lives and, like literature, it always will.

INTRODUCTION

It could be argued that we first correspond with
our mothers from the comfort of the womb, our
earliest letters instantly delivered in the form of
kicks, punches, elbows, shoves and headbutts – a
fittingly bumpy warning that *at least* two human
lives are soon to change immeasurably, and forever.
In some cases, this sets the tone for the entire relationship between mother and child, and marks the
beginning of a lifelong struggle to co-exist; for
others this may be the last exchange they have.
However, for most, this flurry of urgent messages
marks the beginning of a connection that will
remain throughout the lives of those involved, and
in some ways beyond.

Letters of Note: Mothers is a celebration of this most
fundamental and complicated of human bonds by
way of old-fashioned correspondence: a collection
of thirty letters written to, from or about mothers
that may humour, anger, comfort or sadden you
depending on your current situation, the day of the
week, the look your daughter just gave you, the
tone of your mum's latest text, or the entirely
unreasonable manner in which your son emptied

the dishwasher before disappearing upstairs to his bedroom, which, by the way, hasn't been tidied since July, and have I told you about his new tattoo?

The oldest letter in this volume was written in the fourth century AD by a young Egyptian girl mourning her mother's death; the most recent was sent in 2018 by a young English woman who was inspired by the plot of a movie to write to hers. In the years between, you will find a letter from a disappointed mother, sent to an underachieving teenage son who went on to lead his country to victory in World War II; a fiery exchange of letters between a Hollywood leading lady and her daughter, which for some reason they published in their respective memoirs for all to see; a heart-breaking yet beautiful letter from a terminally ill woman to her young daughters, in which she explains her predicament; a farewell letter from a twenty-three-year-old kamikaze pilot to his mother, written a few days before his final mission; and much more.

While researching this book, two things quickly became evident that I think are worth mentioning. The first is that the majority of correspondence from mothers to their children is written when those offspring are very young or even in utero –

hope-filled, brightly lit letters in which these fresh, unblemished humans are welcomed into the world with words of much needed advice. But what I also came to realise is that most missives in the opposite direction, from child to mother, are written at the other end of the life cycle, when those parents are nearing the *end* of their lives or have recently passed away – farewell letters, often laced with regret at not having communicated enough, at times when it mattered.

Put simply – and I apologise for sounding like your mum – let's write more letters to our mothers during the large expanse of time *between* birth and death, when life really happens. Your mother will appreciate it, and so will the next generation when those action-packed letters are handed down.

Now, I need to go. I have a letter to write.

Shaun Usher
2020

The Letters

LETTER 01
YOU ARE AN INSPIRATION
Melissa Rivers to Joan Rivers
2013

On Sunday, 7 September 2014, crowds gathered outside Temple Emanu-El on New York's Fifth Avenue in order to pay their respects to the recently departed Joan Rivers. Born in Brooklyn in 1933 to Russian immigrant parents, Rivers was an outspoken comedian who had been a household name since the 1960s thanks to her numerous television projects. Many speeches were made in memory of Rivers that day, including one by her daughter, Melissa, whose spare room Rivers had stayed in sporadically over the years while filming in Los Angeles. To the delight of all gathered, after saying a few words, Melissa read out this letter, written to her late mother the year before.

THE LETTER

Mom:

I received the note that you slipped under my bedroom door last night. I was very excited to read it, thinking that it would contain amazing, loving advice that you wanted to share with me. Imagine my surprise when I opened it and saw that it began with the salutation, "Dear Landlord." I have reviewed your complaints and address them below:

1. While I appreciate your desire to "upgrade" your accommodations to a larger space, I cannot, in good conscience, move [thirteen-year-old son] Cooper into the laundry room. I do agree that it will teach him a life lesson about fluffing and folding, but since I don't foresee him having a future in dry cleaning, I must say no.

Also, I know you are a true creative genius (and I am in awe of the depth of your instincts), but breaking down a wall without my permission is not an appropriate way to express that creativity. It is not only a boundary violation but a building-code violation as well. Additionally, the repairman can't get here until next week, so your expansion plan will have to be put on hold.

2. Re: Your fellow "tenant" (your word), Cooper. While I trust you with him, it is not OK for you to

undermine my rules. It is not OK that you let him have chips and ice cream for dinner. It is not OK that you let him skip school to go to the movies. And it is really not OK that the movie was *Last Tango in Paris*.

As for your taking his friends to a "gentlemen's club," I accepted your rationale that it was an educational experience for the boys – and you are right, he is the most popular kid in school right now – but I'd prefer he not learn biology from those "gentlemen" and their ladies, Bambi, Trixie and Kitten. And just because I yelled at you, I do not appreciate your claim that I have created a hostile living environment.

3. While I'm glad to see you're socializing, you must refill the hot tub after your parties. In fact, you need to tone down the parties altogether. Imagine my surprise when I saw the photos you posted on Facebook of your friends frolicking topless in the hot tub.

I think it's great that you're entertaining more often, but I can't keep fielding complaints from the neighbors about your noisy party games like Ring Around the Walker or naked Duck, Duck Caregiver.

I'm more than happy to have you use the house for social gatherings, but you cannot rent it out, advertise as "party central" or hand out T-shirts that say "F— Jimmy Buffett."

In closing, I hope I have satisfactorily answered your complaints and queries. I love having you live with me, and I am grateful for every minute Cooper and I have with you. You are an inspiration. You are also 30 days late with the rent.

Much love,
Melissa

LETTER 02
I KNOW, MOTHER, I KNOW
Anne Sexton to Linda Sexton
April 1969

Born in Newton, Massachusetts, in 1928, Anne Sexton battled mental illness for much of her adult life, the births of her two girls in her twenties only serving to deepen and complicate her mental anguish. It was on the advice of her therapist during a stay at hospital in 1955, two years after the birth of her first daughter, Linda, that she began to write the poetry that would keep her suicidal thoughts at bay and give her family and friends hope. While travelling in 1969, two years before she won the Pulitzer Prize for her book, Live or Die, *Sexton wrote to Linda, then fifteen, with a message for the future. Five years after this emotional letter was penned, Sexton finally took her own life. She was forty-five years old.*

THE LETTER

Dear Linda,

I am in the middle of a flight to St. Louis to give a reading. I was reading a *New Yorker* story that made me think of my mother and all alone in the seat I whispered to her "I know, Mother, I know." (Found a pen!) And I thought of you – someday flying somewhere all alone and me dead perhaps and you wishing to speak to me.

And I want to speak back. (Linda, maybe it won't be flying, maybe it will be at your *own* kitchen table drinking tea some afternoon when you are 40. *Anytime.*) – I want to say back.

1st, I love you.

2. You *never* let me down

3. I know. I was there once. I *too*, was 40 and with a dead mother who I needed still.

This is my message to the 40-year-old Linda. No matter what happens you were always my bobolink, my special Linda Gray. Life is not easy. It is awfully lonely. I know that. Now you too know it – wherever you are, Linda, talking to me. But I've had a good life – I wrote unhappy – but I lived to the hilt. You too, Linda – Live to the HILT! To the top. I love you, 40-year old Linda, and I love what you do, what you find, what you are! – Be your own woman. Belong to those you love. Talk to my poems, and talk to your heart – I'm in both: if you need me. I lied, Linda. I did love my mother and she loved me. She never held me but I miss her, so that I have to deny I ever loved her – or she me! Silly Anne! So there!

XOXOXO

Mom

'LIVE TO THE HILT!'

— *Anne Sexton*

LETTER 03
I AM DANNY DEVITO'S MOTHER
Julia DeVito to Kirk Douglas
1973

*In 1973, at the very beginning of Danny DeVito's long
and illustrious movie career, he was cast in Scalawag, a
largely forgotten film directed by, and starring, an
already beloved Hollywood legend, Kirk Douglas. It
received, at best, lukewarm reviews upon release. No
one was prouder of the film, however, than DeVito's
mother, Julia, and soon after watching it she sent an
endearing letter to Douglas to thank him for casting
her son. Julia went on to star alongside her son in the
widely adored sitcom, Taxi. She passed away in 1987.
Kirk Douglas reprinted her charming letter in his auto-
biography a year later, and in 1991 Danny DeVito read
it aloud to an audience of hundreds as the AFI Life
Achievement Award was awarded to Douglas.*

THE LETTER

Dear Mr. & Mrs. Douglas:

I am Danny DeVito's mother, writing to thank you both for giving my son a part in your movie, "Scallywag." My family all went to see it at the Paramount in N.Y.C. it was a great movie. Some of my friends & relatives saw it in Florida, they called me up to-day, to tell me that Danny was great they liked his acting, so that made me feel so proud. Half of Asbury Park N.J. are waiting for it to come here. My daughter owns a Beauty Salon in Neptune N.J. and has a sign in it: "Scallywag Coming Soon." You see there is plenty of publicity out here.

Love to your son Michael, he spent a weekend at our house & we all love him & we also watch the Streets of San Francisco on Thursday nights.

Again, I want to thank you both for giving my son a part in your movie. It's great to have a part with a big star like you.

Sincerely yours,
Mrs. Dan DeVito

LETTER 04
SHINE, CONSTANTLY AND STEADILY
Caitlin Moran to Lizzie Moran
July 2013

British journalist and author Caitlin Moran hails from Brighton, England, the eldest of eight siblings whose working-class family grew up in the English city of Wolverhampton. Since her early teens she has written for a wide audience, and at the age of fifteen was crowned 'Young Reporter of the Year' by the Observer *– the first of many awards she has since received for her work. The mother of two girls herself, in 2013 she wrote this letter to one of her daughters, explaining at the time: 'My daughter is about to turn 13 and I've been smoking a lot recently, and so – in the wee small hours, when my lungs feel like there's a small mouse inside them, scratching to get out – I've thought about writing her one of those "Now I'm Dead, Here's My Letter Of Advice For You To Consult As You Continue Your Now Motherless Life" letters. Here's the first draft. Might tweak it a bit later. When I've had another fag.'*

THE LETTER

Dear Lizzie,

Hello, it's Mummy . . . Look – here are a couple of things I've learnt on the way that you might find useful in the coming years. It's not an exhaustive list, but it's a good start. Also, I've left you loads of life-insurance money – so go hog wild on eBay on those second-hand vintage dresses you like. You have always looked beautiful in them. You have always looked beautiful.

The main thing is just to try to be nice. You already are – so lovely I burst, darling – and so I want you to hang on to that and never let it go. Keep slowly turning it up, like a dimmer switch, whenever you can. Just resolve to shine, constantly and steadily, like a warm lamp in the corner, and people will want to move towards you in order to feel happy, and to read things more clearly. You will be bright and constant in a world of dark and flux, and this will save you the anxiety of other, ultimately less satisfying things like 'being cool', 'being more successful than everyone else' and 'being very thin'.

Second, always remember that, nine times out of ten, you probably aren't having a full-on nervous breakdown – you just need a cup of tea and a biscuit. You'd be amazed how easily and repeatedly you can confuse the two. Get a big biscuit tin.

Three – always pick up worms off the pavement and put them on the grass. They're having a bad day, and they're good for . . . the earth or something (ask Daddy more about this; am a bit sketchy).

Four: choose your friends because you feel most like yourself around them, because the jokes are easy and you feel like you're in your best outfit when you're with them, even though you're just in a T-shirt. Never love someone whom you think you need to mend – or who makes you feel like you should be mended. There are boys out there who look for shining girls; they will stand next to you and say quiet things in your ear that only you can hear and that will slowly drain the joy out of your heart. The books about vampires are true, baby. Drive a stake through their hearts and run away.

Stay at peace with your body. While it's healthy, never think of it as a problem or a failure. Pat your legs occasionally and thank them for being able to run. Put your hands on your belly and enjoy how soft and warm you are – marvel over the world turning over within, the brilliant meat clockwork, as I did when you were inside me and I dreamt of you every night.

Whenever you can't think of something to say in a conversation, ask people questions instead. Even if you're next to a man who collects pre-Seventies screws and bolts, you will probably never have another opportunity to find out so much about pre-Seventies screws and bolts, and you never know when it will be useful.

This segues into the next tip: life divides into AMAZING ENJOYABLE TIMES and APPALLING EXPERIENCES THAT WILL MAKE FUTURE AMAZING ANECDOTES. However awful, you can get through any experience if you imagine yourself, in the future, telling your friends about it as they scream, with increasing disbelief, 'NO! NO!' Even when Jesus was on the cross, I bet He was thinking, 'When I rise in three days, the disciples aren't going to believe this when I tell them about it.'

Babyiest, see as many sunrises and sunsets as you can. Run across roads to smell fat roses. Always believe you can change the world – even if it's only a tiny bit, because every tiny bit needed someone who changed it. Think of yourself as a silver rocket – use loud music as your fuel; books like maps and co-ordinates for how to get there. Host extravagantly, love constantly, dance in comfortable shoes, talk to Daddy and Nancy about me every day and never, ever start smoking. It's like buying a fun baby dragon that will grow and eventually burn down your f***ing house.

Love,

Mummy.

LETTER 05
ISN'T IT BEAUTIFUL, MOTHER?
E.B. White to Stanley Hart White
16 May 1936

Novelist E.B. White once wrote: 'If an unhappy child-
hood is indispensable for a writer, I am ill-equipped.'
His father, Samuel, and mother, Jessie, were forty-five
and forty-one respectively when Elwyn, known in adult
life as Andy, made his unplanned entry into the family,
his older brother Stanley soon taking him under his
wing to teach him practical skills like reading and
handling a pocket knife. After their father died in 1935,
their mother moved to Washington, D.C., to be cared
for by daughter Clara, and died of liver cancer nine
months later, having selflessly devoted her adult life to
her family. After his mother's death, Andy wrote to his
sadly absent brother and described the past few days.

THE LETTER

Dear Bun:

Mother got steadily weaker, and Wednesday I went
to Washington in order to see her for the last time.
I got there in the middle of a thunder storm, the
air very hot and oppressive, and found her hanging
on to life regretfully, aware of the noise and afraid
of the lightning. It seemed as though her suffering
was more than anybody could bear. But the next
day—a clear, cool morning with a fine sparkle—I
went in and found her in a curiously exalted state;
her pains seemed to be gone, and she talked with a
sort of feverish excitement about the experience of
death, which she was anxious to make us believe
(while she still had strength enough to speak) was
beautiful. She was very toxic, and focussed her eyes
only with great effort, but she managed to convince
us that she had achieved a peaceful conclusion.
How much of it was chicanery and how much a
merciful truth, I will never know, but she appeared
to be enjoying a sort of spiritual intoxication. I
said: "Isn't it beautiful, Mother?" (meaning the
weather), and she replied, with astonishing fervor,

"Oh, my, oh, my—it's perfectly beautiful" (meaning death). Clara took her hand and said: "Mother, you're perfectly comfortable, aren't you?" And she replied: "Perfectly comfortable." "And you're perfectly happy?" "Perfectly happy." It was an enormous relief after what we had been going through. From the parochial school across the way, Mother could hear the voices of the children singing, and she spoke of that and of how much it had meant to her. Apparently she thoroughly enjoyed the Catholic symbols, and took great comfort in them—liked the big crucifix at the foot of her bed. Occasionally a shudder of pain would make her twitch, and she would murmur, "Oh, oh oh, oh" quickly adding, for our benefit: "That means nothing at all, that means absolutely nothing at all." Her whole mind seemed to be bent on convincing us that all was well with her. She died that night, around ten o'clock; Clara was with her at the time.

Today she received Burr Davis's extreme unction, with the electric organ, the stale lilies, the old colored servants sitting silent and attentive in the little chapel, together with the neighbors from across the street, the doctor who didn't know she had cancer of the liver, and the minister who was sure her soul would go to heaven. Afterwards we drove wearily out to Ferncliff, stopping for the red lights, listening to anecdotes by the interminable Mr. Scholz. I walked down and found Father's stone, which I think is good. We must get another one like it.

This is a very sketchy account of what has been going on these last few days, but I thought you might like to know at least the bare facts. It seems hardly credible that in the course of a single year, Sam and Jessie have gone from this good life.

Yrs as ever,

Andy

THE DAY AFTER TOMORROW I MUST DIE

Ichizō Hayashi to his mother

March 1945

By October 1944 the Allied forces were advancing on the shrinking Japanese empire. Unwilling to surrender, its only remaining option was a final, desperate attempt to inflict as much pain on the enemy as possible by way of kamikaze pilots – mostly young and inexperienced – trained to deliberately fly their explosive-laden planes into enemy warships. The kamikaze training manual assured pilots that at the moment of death they would see their mothers' faces, and that all the sweetest memories of boyhood would flash before their eyes. Nevertheless, as can be seen in this example, the farewell letters they wrote to their parents commonly featured poignant expressions of fear, regret and longing for home and family.

Ichizō Hayashi, aged twenty-three, died in a suicide attack east of Yorenjima on 12 April 1945.

THE LETTER

Mother,

The time has come when I must give you sad news.

You love me more than I will ever be able to love you. What will you think of this letter? I am desperately sorry.

I have been really happy; perhaps I was too spoilt. But it is not my fault. I loved you, and it was so nice to be petted by you.

I am glad that I was selected as a pilot of a "specialized attack" group, but I can hardly restrain my tears when I think of you.

You did all you could to educate me, to help me to face the future. I am very sad that I must die without having given you anything in exchange— neither happiness nor serenity. I can hardly ask you to make the sacrifice of my life as well, nor to take pride in my death, however glorious it may be. It is better that I should not speak of all that to you.

I never dared to refuse the young girl you intended me to marry. I did not want to lose your affection, and I was so happy to receive your letters.

I would have loved to see you once again and to go to sleep in your arms. But the only place where

I could have met you is Moji. For the day after tomorrow I must leave, the day after tomorrow I must die.

It is possible that I shall fly over Hakata. I will bid you farewell in silence from above the clouds. Mother, you used to dream of a splendid future for me, and I am going to disappoint you. I shall never forget your anxiety when I had to pass examinations. I joined this group in spite of your disapproval, but I can see now that I would have done better to follow your advice.

Try to comfort yourself by remembering that I am a very good pilot, and that it is very rare that a member of the air force with so few hours in the air to his credit is chosen for such a mission.

When I am dead, you will still have Makio. You preferred me because I was the elder, but believe me, Makio is worth far more than I. He is very good at looking after all the family interests. You will also have my sisters Chiyoko and Hiroko, and your grandchildren

Cheer up. My soul will always be near you. Your joys will be mine, but if you are sad, I shall be sorrowful too.

Sometimes I feel tempted to come back to you, but that would be a cowardly action.

When I was baptized the priest said these words

over me: "Renounce your own self." I can remember that very well. I will commit my soul to our Saviour before I die, pierced by American bullets. For everything is in God's hands. There is neither life nor death for those who live in God. Jesus Himself has said: "Thy will be done."

I read the Bible every day. Then I feel very close to you. When I crash to my death, I shall have the Bible and the Book of Psalms in my aircraft. I will also take along the mission badge which the director of the college gave me, and your medal.

Perhaps I did not take that marriage business as seriously as I should have done. I would not like to give the impression that I lacked respect for my betrothed and her family. Could you make her understand that it is better to make an end. I would really have liked to marry her: I would gladly have given you that happiness. I did not have time.

I ask only one thing of you: that you should forgive me. But I can go in peace, for I know that you always forgive me. Mother, how I admire you! You have always been so much braver than I. You are capable of forcing yourself to do painful things, and I find it impossible. Your only fault is that you spoilt me too much. But I myself wanted you to do so and I do not reproach you for that.

When I crash on to the enemy I will pray for

you that all your prayers may be granted. I have
asked Ueno to bring you this letter, but you must
never show it to anybody. I am ashamed of it. I
have the impression that it is not I whom death is
waiting for. When I think that I shall never see you
again, I am overcome with grief.

'I KNOW THAT YOU WILL
ALWAYS FORGIVE ME'

— *Ichizō Hayashi*

LETTER 07
YOUR EAGER MOTHER

Jessie Bernard to her unborn child

1941

Renowned American sociologist and feminist Jessie Bernard studied and taught at a number of institutes up until her retirement in 1964, and it was really only then that she became one of feminism's most important voices through the seminal books and articles for which she is now known, including The Future of Marriage *and* The Female World. *She did much of this as a single parent to her three children following the loss of her husband, Luther, to cancer in 1951, six months after the birth of their third child. In 1941, aged thirty-eight and pregnant with their first, Jessie wrote their unborn daughter a letter. Then, when Dorothy Lee was one month old, she wrote again.*

THE LETTERS

4 May 1941

My dearest,

Eleven weeks from today you will be ready for this outside world. And what a world it is this year! It has been the most beautiful spring I have ever seen . . . aglow with color. The forsythia were yellower and fuller than any I have ever seen. The lilacs were fragrant and feathery, and now the spirea, heavy with their little round blooms, stand like wonderful igloos, a mass of white. I doff my scientific mantle long enough to pretend that Nature is outdoing herself to prepare this earth for you. But also I want to let all this beauty get into my body.

I cannot help but think of that other world. The world of Europe where babies are born to hunger, stunted growth, breasts dried up with anxiety and fatigue. That is part of the picture too. And I sometimes think that while my body in this idyllic spring creates a miracle, forces are at work which within twenty or twenty-five years may be preparing to destroy the creation of my body. My own sweet, the war takes on a terrible new significance when I think of that. I think of all those mothers who carried their precious cargoes so carefully for nine long months—and you have no idea how long nine months can be when you are impatient for the end—lovingly nurtured their babies at their breasts, and watched them grow for twenty years. I think of their anguish when all this comes to naught.

. . . To me the only answer a woman can make to the destructive forces of the world is creation. And the most ecstatic form of creation is the creation of new life. I have so many dreams for you. There are so many virtues I would endow you with if I could. First of all, I would make you tough and strong. And how I have labored at that! I have eaten vitamins and minerals instead of food. Gallons of milk, pounds of lettuce, dozens of eggs . . . hours of sunshine. To make your body a strong one because everything depends on that. I would give you resiliency of body so that all the blows and buffets of this world would leave you still unbeaten. I would have you creative. I would have you a creative scientist. But if the shuffling genes have made of you an artist, that will make me happy too. And even if you have no special talent either artistic or scientific, I would still have you creative no matter what you do. To build things, to make things, to create—that is what I covet for you. If you have a

strong body and a creative mind you will be happy.
I will help in that.

Already I can see how parents long to shield
their children from disappointments and defeat. But
I also know that I cannot re-make life for you. You
will suffer. You will have moments of disappoint-
ment and defeat. You will have your share of
buffeting. I cannot spare you that. But I hope to
help you be such a strong, radiant, self-integrated
person that you will take all this in your stride,
assimilate it, and rise to conquer.

Eleven more weeks. It seems a long time. Until
another time, then, my precious one, I say
good-bye.

Your eager mother

*　*　*

24 August 1941

My dearest daughter,
Now that I have held your earthy little body in my
arms and felt that voracious tug of your hungry
lips at my breast, the earlier letters I wrote to you
in the spring seem rather remote and academic.
Now I am so completely absorbed in your physical
care that the more abstract values in your develop-

ment are crowded out . . .

You nursed with much energy, although there was little milk for you . . . I wanted very much to nurse you completely, but alas I did not have enough milk. So we compromised. I nurse you and then give you a bottle. So far you have shown no objection. Your positive, experimental approach showed up again the other day when we first gave you orange juice from a spoon. You took it joyfully, eagerly. No rejections. No objections. We were delighted with the ease of the new adjustment.

The first few weeks at home have been most difficult for you and for us. I am so terribly inexperienced with babies, I had to learn everything from the beginning. And even yet you baffle me completely. You are not at all a scientific object. A practice which at one moment will cause you to stop crying will have no effect at all the next time. You will be crying violently and then in an instant you stop and all is forgiven. It puzzles me immensely. I wish I understood you better . . .

You seem to have an insatiable curiosity about the world. You love to look at things. Your eyes open very wide and you hold your head up over our shoulders and drink in all the sights. I find you utterly adorable. I sit for hours just watching you sleep, or lie awake in your bed. Just the sight and touch of your little body gives me intense pleasure . . .

Caring for you has absorbed me so completely that I have not been able to think or do anything else. I hope now, however, to get better control over myself. For your sake, as well as for mine. I must not allow you to absorb me completely I must learn to live my own life independently, in order to be a better mother to you.

All my love to you, sweet daughter

LETTER 08
IT'S UP TO YOU NOW
B.D. Hyman and Bette Davis
1980s

*In 1983, at the end of an amazing career during which
she was nominated for a then record-breaking ten
Academy Awards (two of which she won) legendary
Hollywood actress Bette Davis – born Ruth Elizabeth
Davis in 1908 – was diagnosed with breast cancer.
Surgery followed, as did a number of strokes which left
her partially paralysed. Then, in 1985, her daughter,
Barbara, released a controversial book titled* My
Mother's Keeper. *It exposed their troubled relationship,
generally painted Davis in a terrible light, and closed
with a brief letter to her mother. Two years later,
Bette Davis published her memoirs – and at the very
end, for all the world to see, was a reply to her
daughter.*

THE LETTERS

So here it is, Mother, the story of you and me, not as you would have it be but as it really was. You wanted me to be like you, a fighter, but I never wanted to fight. Fighting and grand drama have brought you some kind of satisfaction, I hesitate to say happiness, but they bring me misery. Love and laughter have brought me my happiness, but they bore you to tears. I let you have your way and tried to understand you for all those years because, for the most part, I loved and respected you. My husband clenched his teeth and stayed out of the way most of the time because he loved me and understood my dilemma. He also liked the real you, the Ruth Elizabeth you so seldom exposed to any of us . . .

You've consistently refused to hear me. You tear up letters you don't like without finishing them. You hang up the phone if you don't like the words you hear. You've used friends and lawyers to bring pressure to bear when you've wanted something I've been unwilling to give. You've played many roles during my life, some of them brilliantly, some of them basely, but you were only willing to be yourself for a couple of years some fifteen years ago.

Therefore, Mother, I'm bringing the fight to your doorstep; my word is pledged that it won't be fought on ours again. It seems to me that you have two choices. Neither of them is to say you forgive me for writing this book and only want me to love you . . .

Regard this, Mother, as my cry in the wilderness, to prepare the way and make straight your path. There have been many miracles in my life lately and, if the one for which I now pray should be granted, you'll see that path. All that's asked is that Ruth Elizabeth, no roles and no fantasies, follow it to the door. The door will always be open to her.

* * *

Dear Hyman,

You ended your book with a letter to me. I have decided to do the same.

There is no doubt you have a great potential as a writer of fiction. You have always been a great storyteller. I have often, lo these many years, said to you, "B.D., that is not the way it was. You are imagining things."

Many of the scenes in your book I have played on the screen. It could be you have confused the "me" on the screen with "me" who is your mother.

I have violent objections to your quotes of mine regarding actors I have worked with. For the most part, you have cruelly misquoted me. Ustinov I was thrilled to work with and I have great admiration of him as a person and as an actor. You have stated correctly my reactions to working with Faye Dunaway. She was a most exasperating co-star. But to quote me as having said Sir Laurence Olivier was not a good actor is most certainly one of the figments of your imagination. Few actors have ever reached the towering heights of his performances.

You constantly inform people that you wrote this book to help me understand you and your way of life better. Your goal was not reached. I am now utterly confused as to who you are or what your way of life is.

The sum total of your having written this book is a glaring lack of loyalty and thanks for the very privileged life I feel you have been given.

In one of your many interviews while publicizing your book, you said if you sell your book to TV you feel Glenda Jackson should play me. I would hope you would be courteous enough to ask me to play myself.

I have much to quarrel about in your book. I choose to ignore most of it. But not the pathetic creature you claim I have been because of the fact that I did not play Scarlett in "Gone With the Wind." I could have, but turned it down. Mr. Selznick attempted to get permission from my boss, Jack Warner, to borrow Errol Flynn and Bette Davis to play Rhett Butler and Scarlett. I refused because I felt Errol was not good casting for Rhett. At that time only Clark Gable was right. Therefore, dear Hyman, send me not back to Tara, rather send me back to Witch Way, our home on the beautiful coast of Maine where once lived a beautiful human being by the name of B.D., not Hyman.

As you ended your letter in "My Mother's Keeper" — it's up to you now, Ruth Elizabeth — I am ending my letter to you the same way: It's up to you now, Hyman.

Ruth Elizabeth

P.S. I hope someday I will understand the title "My Mother's Keeper." If it refers to money, if my memory serves me right, I've been your keeper all these many years. I am continuing to do so, as my name has made your book about me a success.

'REGARD THIS, MOTHER,
AS MY CRY IN THE
WILDERNESS'

— B.D. Hyman

LETTER 09
ALL OF US HAVE A ROLE IN LIFE

Queen Esther Gupton Cheatham Jones to Renée
Cheatham Neblett

c. 1996

*Queen Esther Gupton Cheatham Jones was born in
1929 in Boston, Massachusetts, and in 1947 gave birth
to a daughter named Renée. From a young age, Renée
had plans to visit Africa, and in 1989 she moved
permanently to Ghana and founded the Kokrobitey
Institute, an education centre that offers residential
programmes to American students wishing to study
teaching, literacy and public health issues. Up until
Jones's death in 2000, mother and daughter kept in
touch by letter. This is just one.*

THE LETTER

Your correspondence has quite a flattering closing. However, there is no reason for you ever to feel inferior to anyone. Our relationship as mother and daughter is the same as yours and Sukari. Respect for motherhood and experience should be acknowledged, nothing else. All of us have a role in life as Shakespeare said, "We have our own entrances, and our exits." The role assigned can be embellished by one's own conscience and desire, or can be executed simply as duty. My decision to do what I did was because you were my responsibility. I owed you the best I could provide emotionally and financially. The exact same as you did for Sukari and Sékou [Neblett's children]. Mothers do this. I knew you would do something. Your job as mother is one already an accomplished task to be proud of. Your dream and work to build Kobkrobitey is beyond what most people, including myself, could imagine. It's more than having a career. Renée, in some sense we function alike. If we decide to do something, we put it in motion, never stopping to think of any obstacles we will encounter in the process. But for me it is how things get done. If I had stopped to think, would I make class throughout the year because of lupus, it would never have happened. You are independent as I, and I, as independent as Dad. It is inherited—so we live with it. When all is done, it is done and it is done your way. Yes, I do get very frustrated by having limitations because of health problems. The reason for such solitude at times is because the separation provides me with not having to explain my lack of participation. Pity serves no one—only understanding.

This year hopefully will be better, even though my body is beginning to feel the presence of constant pain and the aging process. Yet, there is something within me that wants to continue living life as long as I am able. So maybe I am coming to Ghana October 4, '96 for 5 months, and returning for classes in 1997.

Renée, with Kokrobitey no one will ever see your clear vision as clearly as you. Even with input from others, the onus is on you. Well, I love you and have always been proud of you as a daughter and mother. Give Sukari & Sékou my love.

Love mum

'I OWED YOU THE BEST I
COULD PROVIDE'

— Queen Esther Gupton
Cheatham Jones

SHE WAS MY WHOLE FAMILY
Tarê to her aunt, Horeina
Fourth century AD

*In the Institute of Papyrology at the University of
Paris-Sorbonne, one can find a number of conserved
papyri on which letters were written long ago in a
range of languages. This one was translated from its
original Ancient Greek, and was written in Syria in the
fourth century by a lonely young Egyptian girl whose
mother had recently died.*

THE LETTER

To my lady and much-loved aunt, Tarê, the daughter of your sister Allous, sends you greeting in God.

Before all else I pray to God that these words find you healthy and happy. This is my prayer.

Know, my lady, that my mother, your sister, died during the Paschal feast. When I had my mother at my side, she was my whole family. Since the time she died, I have remained alone with no one in a foreign land. Remember me, please, aunt, as if my mother were still alive, and if you find anyone, send me news.

Give my greetings to all of our family. May the Lord keep keep you safe and healthy for a long, peaceful time, my lady.

IT'S NEVER GOING TO BE EASY
Hannah Woodhead to her mother
January 2018

In 2017 filmmaker Greta Gerwig drew accolades with the release of her award-winning directorial debut, Lady Bird. In the semi-autobiographical coming-of-age tale, protagonist Christine 'Lady Bird' McPherson makes the difficult journey from high school to university while navigating an often turbulent relationship with her mother. In January 2018, having recently watched Lady Bird, British film journalist Hannah Woodhead was inspired to write a letter to her own mother.

THE LETTER

Dear Mum,

There's not an awful lot I remember about our
relationship during the 2005–2010 period, but I
think that's largely because there's not a lot I
remember about that time full stop. I hated being a
teenage girl. I didn't go to school, I didn't eat, I
didn't sleep. It was, all things considered, A Bad
Time. We both know that I've gone to great lengths
to forget the unique brand of hormonal malaise
and indentured depression which overshadowed
that period. I tried everything I could think of to
shrug that burden off my back but always found it
barrelling straight back down the metaphorical hill
of life to crush me all over again. You used to tell
me it gets easier, and I'd scream 'When?!'

In time I got so used to the weight, I'd forget I
was carrying it at all. I started to say 'Something's
wrong with me,' forgetting that a) I was a teenage
girl, so intrinsically there was stormy weather
constantly on the horizon, and b) A chemical
imbalance is not a character flaw. That doesn't mean
it hurts any less, of course, as it hurt when Dad
walked out, as it hurt when we were broke, as it
hurt when I thought I'd be stuck in the town I
hated forever. I still don't buy the idea there's

nothing wrong with me, but I'm slowly coming to terms with the notion that it's the 'wrong' bits which make people interesting in the first place.

I spent many years in the curious adolescent limbo of simultaneously wanting to be both extraordinary and ordinary, caught between a push-pull of 'stand out' and 'fit in'. I was frustrated that no one 'got' me. I think that's why I turned to films, the natural medium of the outsider. When I think about being a teenager, I think about hurting, but I also think about other things too. Like listening to Radio 2 in the car when you drove me to psychiatric appointments. Like the numerous times you came to pick me up because I'd passed out at someone's house party which you didn't know I was at in the first place (sorry about that). Like going to the library on a Friday afternoon to rent a DVD for the weekend. I realised sometime later that you weren't watching because you loved movies (you don't) – you were watching them because you loved spending time with me.

You always believed in me when I didn't believe in myself, and you always said 'I have to, I'm your mum', as if a sense of duty is all that compels a person to act so selflessly – and you really *were* selfless, because we didn't have much, and I know everything you had you gave to me. I'm exhausting, and I'm not easy to love, and when I made it especially difficult, you never stopped trying. Even when I was being a little shit (which I suspect was most of the time).

We both know it's not always easy, it's *never* going to be easy. But thanks, at the very least, for teaching me if you keep going, eventually you might be able to laugh about things. And in the end, laughing about our own mortality, and marvelling at what tiny, insignificant specks of stardust we really are, is the best any of us can really hope for. I'm happy with that.

Love your petulant, troublesome, troubled, and eternally grateful (eldest) daughter,

Hannah

LETTER 12
SHE WOULD HAVE ENJOYED IT
ENORMOUSLY

George Bernard Shaw to Stella Campbell

22 February 1913

*George Bernard Shaw was born in 1856 in Dublin,
Ireland, the youngest of three children to George Carr
Shaw and Lucinda Elizabeth Gurly Shaw. In 1872, when
Shaw's mother, a professional singer, fled her alcoholic
husband with daughters in tow, Shaw remained by his
father's side in Dublin to continue work. In 1876, keen
for a career change, he joined them in London and
slowly evolved into the celebrated playwright and
literary critic we now know – indeed, to this day he is
considered one of the great dramatists. Shaw lived
with his mother, 'without the smallest friction of any
kind', until he was forty-two years old and flew the
nest to begin wedded life with political activist
Charlotte Frances Payne-Townshend. After his mother's
funeral in 1913, Shaw wrote to his friend, the actress
Stella Campbell, and described the scene.*

THE LETTER

The Mitre, Oxford

22nd February 1913

What a day! I must write to you about it, because
there is no one else who didn't hate her mother,
and even who doesn't hate her children. Whether
you are an Italian peasant or a Superwoman I
cannot yet find out; but anyhow your mother was
not the Enemy.

Why does a funeral always sharpen one's sense
of humor and rouse one's spirits? This one was a
complete success. No burial horrors. No mourners
in black, snivelling and wallowing in induced grief.
Nobody knew except myself, Granville Barker and
the undertaker. Since I could not have a splendid
procession with lovely colours and flashing life and
triumphant music, it was best with us three. I
particularly mention the undertaker because the
humor of the occasion began with him. I went
down in the tube to Golders Green with Barker,
and walked to the Crematorium; and there came
also the undertaker presently with his hearse,
which had walked (the horse did) conscientiously
at a funeral pace through the cold; though my

mother would have preferred an invigorating trot. The undertaker approached me in the character of a man shattered with grief; and I, hard as nails and in loyally high spirits (rejoicing irrepressibly in my mother's memory), tried to convey to him that this professional chicanery, as I took it to be, was quite unnecessary.

And lo! it wasn't professional chicanery at all. He had done all sorts of work for her for years, and was actually and really in a state about losing her, not merely as a customer, but as a person he liked and was accustomed to. And the coffin was covered with violet cloth – not black.

I must rewrite that burial service; for there are things in it that are deader than anyone it has ever been read over; but I had it read not only because the parson must live by his fees, but because with all its drawbacks it is the most beautiful thing than can be read as yet. And the parson did not gabble and hurry in the horrible manner common on such occasions. With Barker and myself for his congregation (and Mamma) he did it with his utmost feeling and sincerity. We could have made him perfect technically in two rehearsals; but he was excellent as it was; and I shook his hand with unaffected gratitude in my best manner.

At the passage "earth to earth, ashes to ashes, dust to dust" there was a little alteration of the words to suit the process. A door opened in the wall; and the violet coffin mysteriously passed out through it and vanished as it closed. People think that door the door of the furnace; but it isn't. I went behind the scenes at the end of the service and saw the real thing. People are afraid to see it; but it is wonderful. I found there the violet coffin opposite another door, a real unmistakable furnace door. When it lifted there was a plain little chamber of cement and firebrick. No heat. No noise. No roaring draught. No flame. No fuel. It looked cool, clean, sunny, though no sun could get there. You would have walked in or put your hand in without misgiving. Then the violet coffin moved again and went in feet first. And behold! The feet burst miraculously into streaming ribbons of garnet coloured lovely flame, smokeless and eager, like pentecostal tongues, and as the whole coffin passed in it sprang into flame all over; and my mother became that beautiful fire.

The door fell; and they said that if we wanted to see it all through, we should come back in an hour and a half. I remembered the wasted little figure with the wonderful face, and said "Too long" to myself; but we went off and looked at the Hampstead Garden Suburb (in which I have shares), and telephoned messages to the theatre, and bought books, and enjoyed ourselves generally.

By the way I forgot one incident. Hayden Coffin [the well-known actor and singer] suddenly appeared in the chapel. His mother also. The end was wildly funny, she would have enjoyed it enormously. When we returned we looked down through an opening in the floor to a lower floor close below. There we saw a roomy kitchen, with a big cement table and two cooks busy at it. They had little tongs in their hands, and they were deftly and busily picking nails and scraps of coffin handles out of Mamma's dainty little heap of ashes and samples of bone. Mamma herself being at that moment leaning over beside me, shaking with laughter. Then they swept her up into a sieve, and shook her out; so that there was a heap of dust and a heap of calcined bone scraps. And Mamma said in my ear, "Which of the two heaps is me, I wonder!"

And that merry episode was the end, except for making dust of the bone scraps and scattering them on a flower bed.

O grave, where is thy victory?

. . .

And so goodnight, friend who understands
about one's mother, and other things.

G.B.S.

LETTER 13
YOUR LOVING MOTHER
Mary Isabel Stephens to Margaret Mitchell
23 January 1919

*On 22 January 1919, four months after enrolling at
college in Northampton, Massachusetts, eighteen-
year-old Margaret Mitchell received word that her
mother – noted women's rights campaigner and president of the Georgia Equal Suffrage League – had fallen
ill as a result of a deadly flu pandemic that was
sweeping the globe. Her father instructed her to return
home. A few days later, she did just that, only to be
greeted at the train station by her brother with the
tragic news that their mother had succumbed to pneumonia the day before. As the devastated siblings
travelled home from the station, Mitchell was given
this letter, written by her mother. It would be another
seventeen years before Margaret Mitchell's only novel,
Gone with the Wind, took the literary world by storm.*

THE LETTER

January 23, 1919

Dear Margaret,

I have been thinking of you all day long. Yesterday you received a letter saying I am sick. I expect your father drew the situation with a strong hand and dark colors and I hope I am not as sick as he thought. I have pneumonia in one lung and were it not for flu complications, I would have had more than a fair chance of recovery. But Mrs. Riley had pneumonia in both lungs and is now well and strong. We shall hope for the best but remember, dear, that if I go now it is the best time for me to go.

I should have liked a few more years of life, but if I had had those it may have been that I should have lived too long. Waste no sympathy on me. However little it seems to you I got out of life, I have held in my hands all that the world can give. I have had a happy childhood and married the man I wanted. I had children who loved me, as I have loved them. I have been able to give what will put them on the high road to mental, moral, and perhaps financial success, were I going to give them nothing else.

I expect to see you again, but if I do not I must warn you of one mistake a woman of your temperament might fall into. Give of yourself with both hands and overflowing heart, but give only the excess after you have lived your own life. This is badly put. What I mean is that your life and energies belong first to yourself, your husband and your children. Anything left over after you have served these, give and give generously, but be sure there is no stinting of attention at home. Your father loves you dearly, but do not let the thought of being with him keep you from marrying if you wish to do so. He has lived his life; live yours as best you can. Both of my children have loved me so much that there is no need to dwell on it. You have done all you can for me and have given me the greatest love that children can give to parents. Care for your father when he is old, as I cared for my mother. But never let his or anyone else's life interfere with your real life. Goodbye, darling, and if you see me no more then it may be best that you remember me as I was in New York.

Your Loving Mother

'I HAVE HELD IN MY
HANDS ALL THAT THE
WORLD CAN GIVE'
— Mary Isabel Stephens

LETTER 14
GREAT SPIRIT
Edna St. Vincent Millay to Cora B. Millay
15 June 1921

*Cora Buzzell Millay was an iron-willed lady who
divorced her irresponsible husband to raise their three
daughters on her own terms. It was Cora who encouraged Edna, known as Vincent within the family, to
enter the poetry contest that brought her into the
public eye. She supported Edna unstintingly throughout
the many twists and turns of her life, and was repaid
with the poet's passionate love and devotion. At the
time of this letter, Edna was living in Paris and writing
for Vanity Fair under the pseudonym Nancy Boyd. Cora
later joined her there. She died of a cerebral haemor-
rhage at the age of sixty-eight while working on a
biography of her three gifted daughters, all of whom
achieved success in the arts. She is buried at
Steepletop, Edna's home in upstate New York, as are
two of her daughters, Edna and Norma.*

THE LETTER

Hôtel de I'Intendance
50, rue de l'Université,
Paris. [June 15, 1921]

Dearly Beloved:

I have been doing a lot of work lately, and I have
sent word to Mr. Crowninshield to send a cheque
for a hundred dollars to Kathleen; it is for you,
dear, but I didn't know your new address, and
besides you might have trouble in cashing a cheque
in a new place, and such a little place. I have not
yet got the work done for the Metropolitan but I
have written them about it, so they understand.

Darling, I am so excited about the Chore-Boy,
and all the rest of the wonderful news! Whether or
not the Pictorial Review woman can do with it
what she wants to do, never mind, the thing is
started, and oh, my sweetheart, I am happy, happy,
happy! And I am tickled to death that you've had
your old cute head bobbed. I know it is adorable.
You have such pretty, wavy hair, and so much of it.
It must look very thick now. And you were determined you would do it, you sly old thing. I am all
the time talking about you, and bragging, to one
person or another. I am like the Ancient Mariner,

who had a tale in his heart he must unfold to all. I am always button-holing somebody and saying, "Someday you must meet my mother." And then I am off. And nothing stops me till the waiters close up the café. I do love you so much, my mother.

It is nearly six months now since I saw you. A long time. Mother, do you know, almost all people love their mothers, but I have never met anybody in my life, I think, who loved his mother as much as I love you. I don't believe there ever was anybody who did, quite so much, and quite in so many wonderful ways. I was telling somebody yesterday that the reason I am a poet is entirely because you wanted me to be and intended I should be, even from the very first. You brought me up in the tradition of poetry, and everything I did you encouraged. I can not remember once in my life when you were not interested in what I was working on, or even suggested that I should put it aside for something else. Some parents of children that are "different" have so much to reproach themselves with. But not you, Great Spirit.

I hope you will write me as soon as you get this. If you only knew what it means to me to get letters from any of you three over there. Because no matter how interesting it all is, and how beautiful, and how happy I am, and how much work I get done, I am nevertheless away from home,—home being somewhere near where you are, mother dear.

If I didn't keep calling you mother, anybody reading this would think I was writing to my sweetheart. And he would be quite right.

It's a shame Norma isn't being sent to London, poor little girl. She would love so to get over here, and I know she would like to see me, and London is only seven hours from Paris! Not that I wouldn't like to see her, too, but I was thinking of her end of it.

Allan Macdougall is doing very well over here. He is editing a column rather on the style of F.P.A.'s in the Paris edition of the Chicago Tribune, and people are very enthusiastic about it. I just got a letter from Harrison Dowd, who also is doing very well, playing the piano in a jazz orchestra, which he does inimitably well, in Berlin.

Dearest, it was dreadful that you didn't hear a word from me on your birthday. But I didn't notice it was so near the 10th till too late to get a letter to you, and I couldn't cable you, because I had no idea of your address. Sweetheart, if you expected a cable, and were disappointed, I shall just die. Answer me this, if you were all alone on your birthday, and were lonely. Please tell me about it.

I am sending you a little Paris flower, which is

just an old-fashioned pink, isn't it? It smells very sweet now, but will have no odor, I am afraid, by the time it gets to you. It is one of a handful which I bought today of a little tiny girl outside the Café des Deux Magots on the Boulevard St. Germain. I paid ten sous for the bunch, which is to say in ordinary times about two cents, but now less than a cent. These little bits of girls are always going around the cafés selling little bunches of flowers from baskets which they carry on their arms. They always say when asked the price, "Dix sous," and then one always gives them a whole franc, and they smile shyly with self-controlled pleasure.

Well, dear, this is enough for now. I will write again soon. And you write me. And believe me to be as ever, honored parent, your most obedient humble servant and devoted daughter,

Vincent.

'EVERYTHING I DID YOU
ENCOURAGED'

— Edna St. Vincent Millay

LETTER 15
I HAVE THE BEST MOTHER IN THE WORLD
Martin Luther King Jr. to Alberta King Williams
October 1948

*Few people have fought harder for the plight of
African-Americans than Martin Luther King Jr., a
minister and activist who spent most of his all-too-brief
life leading the civil rights movement only to be
stopped by a bullet in Memphis in 1968. He was born
in Atlanta, Georgia, on 15 January 1929, as Michael
King Jr., and it would be five years until his father,
Reverend Michael King Sr., changed both their fore-
names to Martin. King Jr. adored his mother, Alberta,
and in 1948, during his first term at Crozer Theological
Seminary in Upland, Pennsylvania, he wrote her this
letter and let her know. Tragically, six years after the
death of her son, as she sat at the organ in church,
she was assassinated by a man claiming to be on a
mission from God.*

THE LETTER

Dear Mother,

Your letter was received this morning. I often tell the boys around the campus I have the best mother in the world. You will never know how I appreciate the many kind things you and daddy are doing for me. So far I have gotten the money (5 dollars) every week.

As to my wanting some clippings from the newspapers, I must answer yes. I wondered why you hadn't sent many, especially the Atlanta world.

You stated that my letters aren't newsey enough. Well I dont have much news. I never go anywhere much but in these books. Some times the professor comes in class and tells us to read our [*strikeout illegible*] assignments in Hebrew, and that is really hard.

Do you know the girl I used to date at Spelman (Gloria Royster). She is in school at Temple and I have been to see her twice. Also I met a fine chick in Phila who has gone wild over the old boy. Since Barbor told the members of his church that my family was rich, the girls are running me down. Of course, I dont ever think about them I am to busy studying.

I eat dinner at Barbors home quite often. He is

full of fun, and he has one of the best minds of anybody I have ever met.

I haven't had time to contact any of your friends up this way. Maybe I will get to it pretty soon.

I hope you will explain to the members why I haven't written any of them. I am going to write a letter to the entire church next week. It should be there by the ~~forth~~ [first] Sunday.

I hear from Christine [King's sister] every week. I try to answer her as regularly as possible. I hope she will somehow get adjusted to that accounting.

Rev. Ray was here Friday at the state convention. He told me to come up anytime I get ready. He is looking for you and dad in November.

Well I guess I must go back to studying. Give everybody my Regards.

Your son

M.L.

'I NEVER GO
ANYWHERE MUCH BUT
IN THESE BOOKS'

— Martin Luther King Jr.

LETTER 16
I AM WAITING FOR YOU
Sylvia Plath to Aurelia Plath
23 April 1956

In 1956 American poet Sylvia Plath won a fellowship to study at the University of Cambridge, resulting in her living hundreds of miles from her mother, Aurelia. Their relationship was intense and complicated, the truth of it difficult to discern for the outsider. Sylvia's father, Otto, died when she was eight, after which she made her mother sign a promise never to remarry. Sylvia's one novel, The Bell Jar, *was published in 1963. Patently autobiographical, its unflattering portrayal of the main character's mother did not reflect well on Aurelia; and yet, in Sylvia's letters to her mother, of which there are hundreds, their love for each other can be felt. This particular missive was written during the year of her move to England, following a short trip around Europe, and just as she was falling for Ted Hughes. They would marry two months later. Less than seven years after that, Sylvia Plath took her own life.*

THE LETTER

April 23, 1956

Dearest Mother,

Well, finally the blundering American Express sent
me your letter from Rome . . . our minds certainly
work on the same track!

. . . I have already planned to stay in London
three nights and have written to reserve a room for
us; we'll just eat and talk the day you come, but for
the next two I'll get some theater tickets and we'll
plan jaunts to flowering parks, Piccadilly, Trafalgar
Square . . . walking, strolling, feeding pigeons and
sunning ourselves like happy clams. Then, to
Cambridge, where I have already reserved a room
for you for two nights . . . I have made a contract
with one of my husky men to teach me how to
manage a punt before you come, so you shall step
one afternoon from your room at the beautiful
Garden House Hotel right onto the Cam and be
boated up to Granchester through weeping willows
for tea in an orchard! Worry about nothing. Just let
me know your predilections and it shall be accomplished . . .

You, alone, of all, have had crosses that would
cause many a stronger woman to break under the

69

never-ceasing load. You have borne daddy's long, hard death and taken on a man's portion in your work; you have fought your own ulcer attacks, kept us children sheltered, happy, rich with art and music lessons, camp and play; you have seen me through that black night when the only word I knew was No and when I thought I could never write or think again; and, you have been brave through your own operation. Now, just as you begin to breathe, this terrible slow, dragging pain comes upon you, almost as if it would be too easy to free you so soon from the deepest, most exhausting care and giving of love.

. . . know with a certain knowing that you deserve, too, to be with the loved ones who can give you strength in your trouble: Warren and myself. Think of your trip here as a trip to the heart of strength in your daughter who loves you more dearly than words can say. I am waiting for you, and your trip shall be for your own soul's health and growing. You need . . . a context where all burdens are not on your shoulders, where some loving person comes to heft the hardest, to walk beside you. Know this, and know that it is right you should come. You need to imbibe power and health and serenity to return to your job . . .

I feel with all my joy and life that these are

qualities I can give you, from the fulness and brimming of my heart. So come, and slowly we will walk through green gardens and marvel at this strange and sweet world.

Your own loving sivvy

DEAREST WINSTON, YOU MAKE ME VERY UNHAPPY

Jennie Churchill and Winston Churchill

12 June 1890

*In 1890, fifty long years before he confidently led the
United Kingdom to victory against Nazi Germany in
World War II, future prime minister Winston Churchill
was an easily distracted, underachieving fifteen-year-old
coasting through life at London's Harrow School, where
he boarded full-time during term. In June of that year,
his notoriously strict mother, Lady Randolph Churchill –
whom he claimed to have loved 'dearly, but at a
distance' – came face to face with a school report that
left her feeling less than enthused. Never one to couch
her words, she reacted by way of this typically
unguarded letter to her son, one of many she wrote to
him over the years. Winston's reply came a week later.*

THE LETTERS

June 12, 1890
2 Connaught Place

Dearest Winston,

I am sending this by Everest [Winston's nanny],
who is going to see how you are getting on. I
would go down to you – but I have so many
things to arrange about the Ascot party next week
that I can't manage it.

I have much to say to you, I'm afraid not of a
pleasant nature. You know darling how I hate to
find fault with you, but I can't help myself this
time. In the first place your father is very angry
with you for not acknowledging the gift of the £5
for a whole week, and then writing an offhand
careless letter.

Your report which I enclose is as you will see a
very bad one. You work in such a fitful inharmo-
nious way, that you are bound to come out last
– look at your place in the form! Your father & I
are both more disappointed than we can say. If only
you had a better place in your form & were a little
more methodical I would try to & find an excuse
for you.

Dearest Winston you make me very unhappy – I

had built up such hopes about you & felt so proud of you — & now all is gone. My only consolation is that your conduct is good and you are an affectionate son — but your work is an insult to your intelligence. If you would only trace out a plan of action for yourself & carry it out & be <u>determined</u> to do so — I am sure you could accomplish anything you wished. It is that thoughtlessness of yours which is your greatest enemy.

I will say no more now, but Winston you are old enough to see how serious this is to you — & how the next year or two & the use you make of them, will affect your whole life. Stop & think it out for yourself & take a good pull before it is too late. You know dearest boy that I will always help you all I can.

Your loving but distressed
Mother

* * *

[19 June 1890]
[Harrow]

My darling Mummy
I have not written till now because I can write a much longer letter. I will not try to excuse myself

for not working hard, because I know that what with one thing and another I have been rather lazy. Consequently when the month ended the crash came I got a bad report & got put on reports etc. etc. That is more than 3 weeks ago, and in the coming months I am <u>bound</u> to get a good report as I have had to take daily reports to Mr Davidson twice a week and they have been very good on the whole.

And then about not answering Papa's letter – I did that very evening & I gave it to the Page to put in the Pillar box & a 1^d for him at the same time.

I could not put it there myself because it was after Lock-up. He I suppose forgot and did not post it until several days had elapsed. My own Mummy I can tell you your letter cut me up very much. Still there is plenty of time to the end of term and I will do my <u>very best</u> in what remains. [. . .]

Good Bye, my own,

With love I remain, Your own

Winston S. Churchill

LETTER 18
THE STORY COMES FROM WITHIN YOU
Laura Dern to Jaya Dern
2017

Born to actors Diane Ladd and Bruce Dern in 1967 in Los Angeles, from the age of two Laura Dern lived with and was parented by her mother and grandmother. Having spent much time on the sets of her parents' movies, it seemed natural that Dern would one day follow in their footsteps, and she did exactly that when she made her screen debut at the tender age of six, alongside her mother in the action film White Lightning. *Thanks to roles in films such as* Blue Velvet *and* Jurassic Park, *and the recent television series* Big Little Lies, *she has become a household name. In 2001 she became a mother herself with the birth of a son; three years later she had a daughter. In 2017, with womanhood on her mind, she wrote the following letter to her teenage girl.*

THE LETTER

Dear Jaya,

I've been thinking a lot lately about what it means to be a woman today. A woman in her own skin, in her power, without any labels placed on her. And as part of that process, I've thought back to what I saw when I was your age.

The '70s were a very new time culturally. Unlike women in my grandmother's generation, who were told to choose between just a few life options, my mother and her friends were part of the revolution in which women made clear that they were not satisfied by limitations—they wanted to do it all. Although society was beginning to accept this, it was assumed that those who tried to do it all were going to fail at everything.

So, my reaction, as I got older, was to decide that even though I could do all things, I was going to focus only on one at a time. Continually striving not to fail was the burden I put on myself. And I'm writing this to you because I want to make sure that you don't limit yourself in the same ways.

I've spent a lot of my life going, "OK, I'm going to be an actress, but I have to give it everything, so I probably won't be able to also have a successful relationship," or "I'm about to be a mother, so I'll give up my acting," or "I'm married, so I'm going to put my career on hold and be 'a good wife' and support him."

Most recently, you and I saw a woman running for president, and we were told, "Oh, yeah, she's brilliant, she's presidential, but she's cold, so she's probably not a good wife and mother. She's not compassionate." Why? Because she's brilliant? I know that confused both of us. It should never be the case that defining yourself as one thing lessens your ability to be everything else. In this strange climate I started realising that focusing on one thing in an effort not to fail at anything else was a weight I was carrying. And I want to be a woman who does it all, no matter how it turns out.

Jaya, I've woken to something recently, and it has inspired me during this time in my life. Here it is: Life is scary, and it's glorious. You're never going to get it all right. You'll get it deliciously messed up, and that will be part of figuring out who you are.

There's a huge force that's affecting your genera- tion – it's called social media, and it's mothering you as much as I am. This other mother is very influential, and she's telling you that your value is determined by how many people follow you. She is also deciding what beauty looks like and which extravagances add up to a fun life.

What social media is giving young girls right now are the two stories that keep us trapped – the black and the white. At one extreme, everything's perfect and light, and everyone's surrounded by friends. The other end of the spectrum seems to glamorize the darkest depression and solitude. But I want you to know that most of your life will happen in the gray spaces between bliss and heartbreak, between having everything lock into place and having it all fall apart. That's where the grace is.

I want you to have faith and hear yourself when you're just barely holding it together. I want you to be able to talk to friends about their gray areas and be open about your own without judgment. You will succeed and fail in equal measure. Both experiences are worthwhile. They will both define you. The truth is, the minute I surrendered to the flow of the mess of life, everything came together magnificently: my longing for art, my skill as an actor, and my capacities as a friend and mother.

The beauty of being a woman today is in savoring the minutiae of life, all the moments that add up to you. The joy you'll find in being in your body, in sexuality and sensuality, in service, in art, in mothering. You have to get out of your own way and write your own story—and not be forced into the narrative that you think will give you the easiest path to success or the most likes. I want you to live in the space that's your own, your own delicious mess. The story comes from within you.

Love,
Mom

'LIFE IS SCARY, AND IT'S GLORIOUS'

— Laura Dern

LETTER 19
WHAT IS A MINUTE?
Tina LeBlanc Sadoski and Mister Rogers
17 August 1988

On 19 February 1968 Mister Rogers' Neighborhood *made
its national debut on PBS in the United States, in turn
introducing the nation to its soon-to-be beloved host,
Fred Rogers, an impossibly calm and affable gentleman
who would spend the next thirty-three years educating
millions of children on a plethora of subjects and
become an extra family member in many a household.
Rogers was a man of many talents – responsible not
just for hosting the show, he also produced and wrote
each episode. He even voiced the show's puppets and
composed its music, including the famous theme song,
'Won't You Be My Neighbor?' He also replied to the
thousands of letters he received each year from the
viewers he liked to call his 'television friends'. In
August 1988 he received a letter from a lady named
Tina LeBlanc Sadoski, regarding her daughter who was
in hospital. Rogers soon replied, both to mother and
daughter, and wrote many more times as the young
girl's treatment continued. Sadly, Michelle Sadoski died
in January 1990.*

THE LETTERS

Dear Mister Rogers,

Our 5½-year-old daughter, Michelle, has an inoperable brain tumor. Our only hope to remove the tumor is with radiation. On the first day of her radiation treatment, she screamed and cried when she found out she would have to be in the room all by herself. She was so upset they could not give her the treatment.

The next day the doctor gave us some medication to sedate her. It was supposed to put her to sleep. By the time we reached the hospital she was still wide awake. We all tried talking her into doing the treatment, but she cried again and said no. We kept saying that it would only take one minute-thirty seconds on each side.

Finally she asked me, "What is a minute?" I know it was by the grace of God that I thought of how to explain to her what was one minute. I looked at my watch and started singing, "It's a beautiful day in this neighborhood, a beautiful day for a neighbor . . ." and before I could finish the song I said, "Oops! The minute is up. I can't even finish Mr. Rogers' song." Then Michelle said, "Is that a minute? I can do that." And she did. She laid perfectly still for the entire treatment, but, there was a catch to it. I have to sing your song every time over the intercom into the treatment room. It is very embarrassing, but I do it gladly for her. By now, every doctor and technician in Radiation Therapy knows your song.

I just wanted to share this with you and to let you know what a wonderful job you are doing for all children. You touch their lives in more ways than you realize.

Michelle's Mom

* * *

MISTER ROGERS'
NEIGHBORHOOD

August, 1988

Dear Michelle,
It was good to get to know you from your mother's letter. I am glad that you enjoy our television visits so much.

Your mother told me that you have cancer and needed to have radiation treatment. It can be hard to manage with a lot of things at the hospital. Michelle, I hope that you can talk about what you're feeling with the people in your family and with the people at the hospital – when you're angry or sad or scared or happy. I call that "important talk".

It meant a lot to me to know that our song "Won't You Be My Neighbor" helped you so much during the radiation treatment. I wanted to send you an audio tape of that, along with some other gifts. And I will think of you when I sing that song.

Michelle, there are a lot of people who care about you. Your family cares about you. The people at the hospital care about you. And I care about you as a television friend. You make each day special for the people who care about you – just because you're you.

All of us here in the Neighborhood send our best wishes to you.

Your television friend,
Mister Rogers

LETTER 20
MATERNAL LOVE REQUIRES NO REASONS
Richard Wagner to Johanna Wagner
25 July 1835

German composer Richard Wagner was just six months old when his father died, leaving his mother, Johanna, alone with their nine children. Wagner's mother doubted his musical talent and encouraged him to pursue a traditional education, but he was an indifferent student and threw himself into a dissolute lifestyle of drinking, gambling and debauchery. He hit rock bottom one night after gambling away his mother's pension and winning it back, before confessing all to her and vowing to change his ways. He wrote this letter when he was twenty-two. She died in 1848, having lived long enough to see her youngest son achieve some modest success in his chosen field, and just months before he completed the first draft of the libretto for his epic operatic cycle The Ring of the Nibelung.

THE LETTER

Carlsbad, the 25th July :35.

Only of yourself, dearest Mother, can I think with
the sincerest love and profoundest emotion.
Brothers and sisters, I know it, must go their own
way,—each has an eye to himself, to his future, and
the surroundings connected with both. So it is, and
I feel it myself: there comes a time when roads
part of themselves, — when our mutual relations
are governed solely from the standpoint of external
life; we become mere nodding diplomats to one
another, keeping silence where silence seems
politic, and speaking where our view of an affair
demands; and when we're at a distance from each
other, we speak the most. But ah, how high a
mother's love is poised above all that!

No doubt I, too, belong to those who cannot
always speak out at the moment as their heart
dictates,—or you might often have come to know
me from a much more melting side. But my senti-
ments remain the same,—and see, Mother— now I
have left you, the feeling of thanks for that grand
love of yours towards your child, which you
displayed to him so warmly and so tenderly again
the other day, so overpowers me that I fain would

write, nay, tell you of it in accents soft as of a lover to his sweetheart. Yes, and still softer,—for is not a mother's love far more—far more untainted than all other?

Nay, here I won't philosophise,—I simply want to thank you, and again, to thank you,—and how gladly would I count up all the separate proofs of love for which I thank,—were there not too many of them. O yes, I know full well that no heart yearns after me now with so great an inner sympathy or such solicitude, as yours; yes, that perhaps it is the only one that watches o'er my every step,—and not, forsooth, coldly to criticise it,—no, to include it in your prayers. Have you not ever been the only one to stay unalterably true to me when others, judging by mere outward results, turned philosophically away? It would indeed be exacting beyond measure, were I to ask a like affection from them all; I even know it is not possible,—I know it from myself: but with you all issues from the heart, that dear good heart I pray God e'er to keep inclined to me,—for I know that, should all else forsake me, 'twould still remain my last, my fondest refuge. O Mother, what if you should prematurely die, ere I had fully proved to you that it was to a worthy son, of boundless gratitude, you shewed so great a love! But no, that cannot be; you still must taste abundant fruits. Ah, the remembrance of that latest week with you; it is a perfect feast to me, a cordial, to call before my soul each several token of your loving care! My dear, dear Mother,—what a wretch were I, if I could ever cool towards thee!

For the future I shall tell the family but little of my doings,—they judge by the outward results, and will learn those without my assistance. In whatever fashion it has come about, I'm independent now, and mean to stay so. O that humbling before Brockhaus is graven deep into my heart, and the bitterest self—reproaches torture me, that I should have given into his hands a right to humble me. I shall get even with him in time, but never, never at one with him; and should that be wrong of me, I prefer to bear that wrong into the grave with me: I withdraw from them entirely. Each side cannot be right, and I was wrong ;—yet I will never admit it—to them, but place myself in such a situation that I've nothing to admit to them,— whereas my recent great fault was having played into their hands, given them the very smallest right against me. For that matter, we stand so far from one another, that it would be absurd of me to want to be at one with him. Yet, how I do rejoice at this catastrophe, which has brought me full recognition that I have nothing to expect from anybody in this world, but must stand on my own pair of feet! I feel independent at last, It was this feeling I lacked, and that lack which made me negligent and easy-going;—I had a certain vague reliance on some backer, which foolishly did not restrict itself to Apel, but also took other fantastic directions that almost make me laugh at my stupidity. Now I'm undeceived about all that, and very glad to be. My softness needed these experiences,—which will profit me in every way. Only, I straightway beg them to deny me any sympathy,—'twould irk me; —yourself, your heart, your love shall be my only stand-by, my refuge and hope in every trouble of my coming life. Maternal love requires no reasons,—all other seeks to fathom why it loves, and therefore turns to nothing but regard.

I have been to Teplitz and Prague, and found nothing there beyond the confirmation of my plan not to go to Vienna, and advice to pursue the direction I already have struck. Moritz was in Prague, and gave me many a hint in this respect. From Prague I wrote to all the individuals I have my eye on, so as to know beforehand where I stand with them, and take no road in vain. I am expecting their answers at Nuremberg, whither I go to-morrow or the next day, as I'm only waiting for a letter from Magdeburg to conclude my business here. I shall make a halt at Nuremberg; when a company is being disbanded, one easily picks something up;—moreover, the Wolframs can give me a deal of information, so that their opinion, perhaps, will save me a journey or two.

My dear, dear Mother,—my good angel,—fare heartily well, and don't fret;—you have a grateful son who never, never will forget what you are to him.—With the tenderest remembrances, Thy
RICHARD.

LETTER 21
LIVE A LIFE WORTH LIVING
Julie Yip-Williams to Mia and Isabelle
July 2017

On 19 March 2018, almost five years after being diag-
nosed with Stage IV colon cancer, thirty-eight-year-old
Julie Yip-Williams died, leaving behind a husband and
two daughters. Her early years had been anything but
easy. Born blind in Vietnam, at two months of age she
was almost euthanised on the orders of a grandmother
who deemed her to be defective; years later, as an
older child, she sailed to Hong Kong with her family
and hundreds of other refugees in search of a more
peaceful life, eventually settling down in the US where
her life improved drastically. She was soon given
partial sight by a surgeon, studied at Harvard, and
became a successful lawyer, but then, in her thirties,
she was struck down by the illness that would kill her.
It was then she began writing a popular blog about
her experience with cancer, which was posthumously
published as a memoir. A year before she passed away,
Yip-Williams wrote a letter to her young daughters.

THE LETTER

Dear Mia and Isabelle,

I have solved all the logistical problems resulting
from my death that I can think of – I am hiring a
very reasonably priced cook for you and Daddy; I
have left a list of instructions about who your
dentist is and when your school tuition needs to be
paid and when to renew the violin rental contract
and the identity of the piano tuner. In the coming
days, I will make videos about all the ins and outs
of the apartment, so that everyone knows where
the air filters are and what kind of dog food
Chipper eats. But I realized that these things are the
low-hanging fruit, the easy-to-solve but relatively
unimportant problems of the oh so mundane.

I realized that I would have failed you greatly as
your mother if I did not try to ease your pain from
my loss, if I didn't at least attempt to address what
will likely be the greatest question of your young
lives. You will forever be the kids whose mother
died of cancer, have people looking at you with
some combination of sympathy and pity (which
you will no doubt resent, even if everyone means
well). That fact of your mother dying will weave
into the fabric of your lives like a glaring stain on
an otherwise pristine tableau. You will ask as you

look around at all the other people who still have their parents, Why did my mother have to get sick and die? It isn't fair, you will cry. And you will want so painfully for me to be there to hug you when your friend is mean to you, to look on as your ears are being pierced, to sit in the front row clapping loudly at your music recitals, to be that annoying parent insisting on another photo with the college graduate, to help you get dressed on your wedding day, to take your newborn babe from your arms so you can sleep. And every time you yearn for me, it will hurt all over again and you will wonder why.

I don't know if my words could ever ease your pain. But I would be remiss if I did not try.

My seventh-grade history teacher, Mrs. Olson, a batty eccentric but a phenomenal teacher, used to rebut our teenage protestations of "That's not fair!" (for example, when she sprang a pop quiz on us or when we played what was called the "Unfair" trivia game) with "Life is not fair. Get used to it!" Somehow, we grow up thinking that there should be fairness, that people should be treated fairly, that there should be equality of treatment as well as opportunity. That expectation must be derived from growing up in a rich country where the rule of law is so firmly entrenched. Even at the tender age of five, both of you were screaming about fairness as if it were some fundamental right (as in it wasn't fair that Belle got to go to see a movie when Mia did not). So perhaps those expectations of fairness and equity are also hardwired into the human psyche and our moral compass. I'm not sure.

What I do know for sure is that Mrs. Olson was right. Life is not fair. You would be foolish to expect fairness, at least when it comes to matters of life and death, matters outside the scope of the law, matters that cannot be engineered or manipulated by human effort, matters that are distinctly the domain of God or luck or fate or some other unknowable, incomprehensible force.

Although I did not grow up motherless, I suffered in a different way and understood at an age younger than yours that life is not fair. I looked at all the other kids who could drive and play tennis and who didn't have to use a magnifying glass to read, and it pained me in a way that maybe you can understand now. People looked at me with pity, too, which I loathed. I was denied opportunities, too; I was always the scorekeeper and never played in the games during PE. My mother didn't think it worthwhile to have me study Chinese after English school, as my siblings did, because she assumed I wouldn't be able to see the characters. (Of course, later on, I would study Chinese throughout college and study abroad and my Chinese would surpass my siblings'.) For a child, there is nothing worse than being different, in that negative, pitiful way. I was sad a lot. I cried in my lonely anger. Like you, I had my own loss, the loss of vision, which involved the loss of so much more. I grieved. I asked why. I hated the unfairness of it all.

My sweet babies, I do not have the answer to the question of why, at least not now and not in this life. But I do know that there is incredible value in pain and suffering, if you allow yourself to experience it, to cry, to feel sorrow and grief, to hurt. Walk through the fire and you will emerge on the other end, whole and stronger. I promise. You will ultimately find truth and beauty and wisdom and peace. You will understand that nothing lasts forever, not pain, or joy. You will understand that joy cannot exist without sadness. Relief cannot exist without pain. Compassion cannot exist without cruelty. Courage cannot exist without fear. Hope cannot exist without despair. Wisdom cannot exist without suffering. Gratitude cannot exist without deprivation. Paradoxes abound in this life. Living is an exercise in navigating within them.

I was deprived of sight. And yet, that single unfortunate physical condition changed me for the better. Instead of leaving me wallowing in self-pity, it made me more ambitious. It made me more resourceful. It made me smarter. It taught me to ask for help, to not be ashamed of my physical shortcoming. It forced me to be honest with myself and my limitations, and eventually to be honest with others. It taught me strength and resilience.

You will be deprived of a mother. As your mother, I wish I could protect you from the pain. But also as your mother, I want you to feel the pain, to live it, embrace it, and then learn from it. Be stronger people because of it, for you will know that you carry my strength within you. Be more compassionate people because of it; empathize with those who suffer in their own ways. Rejoice in life and all its beauty because of it; live with special zest and zeal for me. Be grateful in a way that only someone who lost her mother so early can, in your understanding of the precariousness and precious-ness of life. This is my challenge to you, my sweet girls, to take an ugly tragedy and transform it into a source of beauty, love, strength, courage, and wisdom.

Many may disagree, but I have always believed, always, even when I was a precocious little girl crying alone in my bed, that our purpose in this life is to experience everything we possibly can, to understand as much of the human condition as we can squeeze into one lifetime, however long or short that may be. We are here to feel the complex range of emotions that come with being human. And from those experiences, our souls expand and grow and learn and change, and we understand a little more about what it really means to be human. I call it the evolution of the soul. Know that your mother lived an incredible life that was filled with more than her "fair" share of pain and suffering, first with her blindness and then with cancer. And I allowed that pain and suffering to define me, to change me, but for the better.

In the years since my diagnosis, I have known love and compassion that I never knew possible; I have witnessed and experienced for myself the deepest levels of human caring, which humbled me to my core and compelled me to be a better person. I have known a mortal fear that was crushing, and yet I overcame that fear and found courage. The lessons that blindness and then cancer have taught me are too many for me to recount here, but I hope, when you read what follows, you will understand how it is possible to be changed in a positive way by tragedy and you will learn the true value of suffering. The worth of a person's life lies not in the number of years lived; rather it rests on how well that person has absorbed the lessons of that life, how well that person has come to understand and distill the multiple, messy aspects of the human experience. While I would have chosen to stay with you for much longer had the choice been mine, if you can learn from my death, if you accepted my challenge to be better people because of my death, then that would bring my spirit inordinate joy and peace.

You will feel alone and lonely, and yet, understand that you are not alone. It is true that we walk this life alone, because we feel what we feel singularly and each of us makes our own choices. But it is possible to reach out and find those like you, and in so doing you will feel not so lonely. This is another one of life's paradoxes that you will learn to navigate. First and foremost, you have each other to lean on. You are sisters, and that gives you a bond of blood and common experiences that is like no other. Find solace in one another. Always forgive and love one another. Then there's Daddy. Then there are Titi and Uncle Mau and Aunt Nancy and Aunt Caroline and Aunt Sue and so many dear friends, all of whom knew and loved me so well – who think of you and pray for you and worry about you. All of these people's loving energy surrounds you so that you will not feel so alone.

And last, wherever I may go, a part of me will always be with you. My blood flows within you. You have inherited the best parts of me. Even though I won't physically be here, I will be watching over you.

Sometimes, when you practice your instruments, I close my eyes so I can hear better. And when I do, I am often overcome with this absolute knowing that whenever you play the violin or the piano, when you play it with passion and commitment, the music with its special power will beckon me and I will be there. I will be sitting right there, pushing you to do it again and again and again, to count, to adjust your elbow, to sit properly. And then I will hug you and tell you how you did a great job and how very proud I am of you. I promise. Even long after you have chosen to stop playing, I will still come to you in those extraordinary and ordinary moments in life when you live with a complete passion and commitment. It might be while you're standing atop a mountain, marveling at exceptional beauty and filled with pride in your ability to reach the summit, or when you hold your baby in your arms for the first time or when you are crying because someone or something has broken your tender heart or maybe when you're miserably pulling an all-nighter for school or work. Know that your mother once felt as you feel and that I am there hugging you and urging you on. I promise.

I have often dreamed that when I die, I will finally know what it would be like to see the world without visual impairment, to see far into the distance, to see the minute details of a bird, to drive a car. Oh, how I long to have perfect vision, even after all these years without. I long for death to make me whole, to give me what was denied me in this life. I believe this dream will come true. Similarly, when your time comes, I will be there waiting for you, so that you, too, will be given what was lost to you. I promise. But in the meantime, live, my darling babies. Live a life worth living. Live thoroughly and completely, thoughtfully, gratefully, courageously, and wisely. Live!

I love you both forever and ever, to infinity, through space and time. Never ever forget that.

Mommy

LETTER 22
PLEASE TELL YOUR MOTHER

G.K. Chesterton to Marie Louise Chesterton

1900

In 1900, twenty-six-year-old English author Gilbert
Keith Chesterton found himself faced with a problem:
he was deeply in love with a lady named Frances
Blogg, and had been for some time, and in fact was so
fond of her that he wished to marry her. However, his
mother, a formidable character, had other ideas: so
much so that she had already chosen his wife – her
friend's angelic daughter, Annie Firmin. And so, one
day, as he sat opposite his mother at the kitchen
table, he wrote her a letter in which his predicament
was explained. It must have worked, as G.K.
Chesterton and Frances Blogg married the next year.
They stayed together until Chesterton's death in 1936.

THE LETTER

1 Rosebery Villas
Granville Road
Felixstowe.

My Dearest Mother,

You may possibly think this is a somewhat eccentric proceeding. You are sitting opposite and talking – about Mrs. Berline. But I take this method of addressing you because it occurs to me that you might possibly wish to turn the matter over in your mind before writing or speaking to me about it.

I am going to tell you the whole of a situation in which I believe I have acted rightly, though I am not absolutely certain, and to ask for your advice on it. It was a somewhat complicated one, and I repeat that I do not think I could rightly have acted otherwise, but if I were the greatest fool in the three kingdoms and had made nothing but a mess of it, there is one person I should always turn to and trust. Mothers know more of their son's idiocies than other people can, and this has been peculiarly true in your case. I have always rejoiced at this, and not been ashamed of it: this has always been true and always will be. These things are easier written than said, but you know it is true, don't you?

I am inexpressibly anxious that you should give me credit for having done my best, and for having constantly had in mind the way in which you would be affected by the letter I am now writing. I do hope you will be pleased.

Almost eight years ago, you made a remark — this may show you that if we "jeer" at your remarks, we remember them. The remark applied to the hypothetical young lady with whom I should fall in love and took the form of saying, "If she is good, I shan't mind who she is." I don't know how many times I have said that over to myself in the last two or three days in which I have decided on this letter.

Do not be frightened; or suppose that anything sensational or final has occurred. I am not married, my dear mother, neither am I engaged. You are called to the council of chiefs very early in its deliberations. If you don't mind I will tell you, briefly, the whole story.

You are, I think, the shrewdest person for seeing things whom I ever knew: consequently I imagine that you do not think that I go down to Bedford Park every Sunday for the sake of the scenery. I should not wonder if you know nearly as much about the matter as I can tell in a letter. Suffice it to say, however briefly (for neither of us care much for gushing: this letter is not on Mrs. Ratcliffe lines) that the first half of my time of acquaintance with the Bloggs was spent in enjoying a very intimate, but quite breezy and Platonic friendship with Frances Blogg, reading, talking and enjoying life together, having great sympathies on all subjects; and the second half in making the thrilling, but painfully responsible discovery that Platonism, on my side, had not the field by any means to itself. That is how we stand now. No one knows, except her family and yourself. My dearest mother, I am sure you are at least not unsympathetic.

Indeed we love each other more than we shall either of us ever be able to say. I have refrained from sentiment in this letter – for I don't think you like it much. But love is a very different thing from sentiment and you will never laugh at that. I will not say that you are sure to like Frances, for all young men say that to their mothers, quite naturally, and their mothers never believe them, also, quite naturally. Besides, I am so confident, I should like you to find her out for yourself. She is, in reality, very much the sort of woman you like, what is called, I believe, "a Woman's Woman," very humorous, inconsequent and sympathetic and defiled with no offensive exuberance of good health.

I have nothing more to say, except that you and she have occupied my mind for the last week to the exclusion of everything else, which must account for my abstraction, and that in her letter she sent the following message: "Please tell your mother soon. Tell her I am not so silly as to expect her to think me good enough, but really I will try to be."

An aspiration which, considered from my point of view, naturally provokes a smile.

Here you give me a cup of cocoa. Thank you.

Believe me, my dearest mother,

Always your very affectionate son,

Gilbert.

'MOTHERS KNOW MORE
OF THEIR SON'S
IDIOCIES THAN OTHER
PEOPLE CAN'

– G.K. Chesterton

LETTER 23
I SHALL ALWAYS BE WITH YOU
Milada Horáková to Jana Horáková
26 June 1950

On 8 June 1950, nine months after being arrested by the Czech secret police on suspicion of leading a plot to overthrow the Communist regime, forty-eight-year-old socialist politician Milada Horáková was found guilty of 'high treason' following a show trial that was broadcast on national radio, and in which she remained defiant. On the 27th of that month, despite international outcry and a petition signed by, amongst others, Albert Einstein and Winston Churchill, Milada Horáková was executed at Prague's Pankrác Prison. The night before her death, she wrote a letter to her sixteen-year-old daughter, Jana. In 1991 President Václav Havel posthumously awarded Horáková the Order of Tomáš Garrigue Masaryk (1st Class).

THE LETTER

My only little girl Jana,
God blessed my life as a woman with you. As your
father wrote in the poem from a German prison,
God gave you to us because he loved us. Apart
from your father's magic, amazing love you were
the greatest gift I received from fate. However,
Providence planned my life in such a way that I
could not give you nearly all that my mind and my
heart had prepared for you. The reason was not that
I loved you little; I love you just as purely and
fervently as other mothers love their children. But I
understood that my task here in the world was to
do you good by seeing to it that life becomes
better, and that all children can live well. And
therefore, we often had to be apart for a long time.
It is now already for the second time that Fate has
torn us apart. Don't be frightened and sad because
I am not coming back any more. Learn, my child,
to look at life early as a serious matter. Life is hard,
it does not pamper anybody, and for every time it
strokes you it gives you ten blows. Become accustomed to that soon, but don't let it defeat you.
Decide to fight. Have courage and clear goals and
you will win over life. Much is still unclear to your
young mind, and I don't have time left to explain

to you things you would still like to ask me. One day, when you grow up, you will wonder and wonder, why your mother who loved you and whose greatest gift you were, managed her life so strangely. Perhaps then you will find the right solution to this problem, perhaps a better one than I could give you today myself. Of course, you will only be able to solve it correctly and truthfully by knowing very, very much. Not only from books, but from people; learn from everybody, no matter how unimportant! Go through the world with open eyes, and listen not only to your own pains and interests, but also to the pains, interests and longings of others. Don't ever think of anything as none of your business. No, everything must interest you, and you should reflect about everything, compare, compose individual phenomena. Man doesn't live in the world alone; in that there is great happiness, but also a tremendous responsibility. That obligation is first of all in not being and not acting exclusive, but rather merging with the needs and the goals of others. This does not mean to be lost in the multitude, but it is to know that I am part of all, and to bring one's best into that community. If you do that, you will succeed in contributing to the common goals of human society. Be more aware of one principle than I have been: approach everything in life constructively – beware of unnecessary negation – I am not saying all negation, because I believe that one should resist evil. But in order to be a truly positive person in all circumstances, one has to learn how to distinguish real gold from tinsel. It is hard, because tinsel sometimes glitters so dazzlingly. I confess, my child, that often in my life I was dazzled by glitter. And sometimes it even shone so falsely, that one dropped pure gold from one's hand and reached for, or ran after, false gold. You know that to organize one's scale of values well means to know not only oneself well, to be firm in the analysis of one's character, but mainly to know the others, to know as much of the world as possible, its past, present, and future development. Well, in short, to know, to understand. Not to close one's ears before anything and for no reason – not even to shut out the thoughts and opinions of anybody who stepped on my toes, or even wounded me deeply. Examine, think, criticize, yes, mainly criticize yourself don't be ashamed to admit a truth you have come to realize, even if you proclaimed the opposite a little while ago; don't become obstinate about your opinions, but when you come to consider something right, then be so definite that you can fight and die for it. As Wolker said, death is not bad. Just avoid gradual dying which is what happens when one suddenly finds oneself apart from the real life of the others. You have to put down your roots where fate determined for you to live. You have to find your own way. Look for it independently, don't let anything turn you away from it, not even the memory of your mother and father. If you really love them, you won't hurt them by seeing them critically – just don't go on a road which is wrong, dishonest and does not harmonize with life. I have changed my mind many times, rearranged many values, but, what was left as an essential value, without which I cannot imagine my life, is the freedom of my conscience. I would like you, my little girl, to think about whether I was right.

Another value is work. I don't know which to assign the first place and which the second. Learn to love work! Any work, but one you have to know really and thoroughly. Then don't be afraid of any thing, and things will turn out well for you.

And don't forget about love in your life. I am not only thinking of the red blossom which one day will bloom in your heart, and you, if fate favors you, will find a similar one in the heart of another person with whose road yours will merge. I am thinking of love without which one cannot live happily. And don't ever crumble love – learn to give it whole and really. And learn to love precisely those who encourage love so little – then you won't usually make a mistake. My little girl Jana, when you will be choosing for whom your maiden heart shall burn and to whom to really give yourself remember your father.

I don't know if you will meet with such luck as I, I don't know if you will meet such a beautiful human being, but choose your ideal close to him. Perhaps you, my little one, have already begun to understand, and now perhaps you understand to the point of pain what we have lost in him. What I find hardest to bear is that I am also guilty of that loss.

Be conscious of the great love and sacrifice Pepik and Veruska are bringing you. You not only have to be grateful to them . . . you must help them build your common happiness positively, constructively. Always want to give them more for the good they do for you. Then perhaps you will be able to come to terms with their gentle goodness.

I heard from my legal representative that you are doing well in school, and that you want to continue . . . I was very pleased. But even if you would one day have to leave school and to work for your livelihood, don't stop learning and studying. If you really want to, you will reach your goal.

I would have liked for you to become a medical doctor – you remember that we talked about it. Of course you will decide yourself and circumstances will, too. But if you stand one day in the traditional alma mater and carry home from graduation not only your doctor's diploma, but also the real ability to bring people relief as a doctor – then, my little girl . . . your mother will be immensely pleased . . . But your mother would only be . . . truly happy, no matter where you stand, whether at the operating table, at the . . . lathe, at your child's cradle or at the work table in your household, if you will do your work skillfully, honestly, happily and with your whole being. Then you will be successful in it. Don't be demanding in life, but have high goals. They are not exclusive of each other, for what I call demanding are those selfish notions and needs. Restrict them yourself. Realize that in view of the disaster and sorrow which happened to you, Vera, Pepicek, grandmother and grandfather . . . and many others will try to give you what they have and what they cannot afford. You should not only not ask them for it, but learn to be modest. If you become used to it, you will not be unhappy because of material things you don't have. You don't know how free one feels if one trains oneself in modesty . . . how he/she gets a head start over against the feeble and by how much one is safer and stronger. I really tried this out on myself. And, if you can thus double your strength, you can set yourself courageous, high goals . . . Read much, and study languages. You will thereby broaden your life and multiply its content. There was a time in my life when I read voraciously, and then again times when work did not permit me to take a single book in my hand, apart from professional literature. That was a shame. Here in recent months I have been reading a lot, even books which probably would not interest me outside, but it is a big and important task to read everything valuable, or at least much that is. I shall write down for you at the end of this letter what I have read in recent months. I am sure you will think of me when you will be reading it.

And now also something for your body. I am glad that you are engaged in sports. Just do it systematically. I think that there should be rhythmic exercises, and if you have time, also some good, systematic gymnastics. And those quarter hours every morning! Believe me finally that it would save you a lot of annoyance about unfavorable proportions of your waist, if you could really do it. It is also good for the training of your will and perseverance. Also take care of your complexion regularly – I do not mean makeup, God forbid, but healthy daily care. And love your neck and feet as you do your face and lips. A brush has to be your good friend, every day, and not only for your hands and feet; use it on every little bit of your skin. Salicyl alcohol and Fennydin, that is enough for beauty, and then air and sun. But about that you will find better advisors than I am.

Your photograph showed me your new hairdo; it looks good, but isn't it a shame to hide your nice forehead? And that lady in the ball gown! Really, you looked lovely, but your mother's eye noticed one fault, which may be due to the way you were placed on the photograph – wasn't the neck opening a little deep for your sixteen years? I am sorry I did not see the photo of your new winter coat. Did you use the muff from your aunt as a fur collar? Don't primp, but whenever possible, dress carefully and neatly. And don't wear shoes until they are run down at the heel! Are you wearing innersoles? And how is your thyroid gland? These questions don't, of course, require an answer, they are only meant as your mother's reminders.

In Leipzig in prison I read a book – the letters of Maria Theresa to her daughter Marie Antoinette. I was very much impressed with how this ruler showed herself to be practical and feminine in her advice to her daughter. It was a German original, and I don't remember the name of the author. If you ever see that book, remember that I made up my mind at that time that I would also write you such letters about my experiences and advice. Unfortunately I did not get beyond good intentions.

Janinko, please take good care of Grandfather Kral and Grandmother Horakova. Their old hearts now need the most consolation. Visit them often and let them tell you about your father's and mother's youth, so that you can preserve it in your mind for your children. In that way an individual becomes immortal, and we shall continue in you and in the others of your blood.

And one more thing – music. I believe that you will show your gratitude to Grandfather Horak for the piano which he gave you by practicing honestly, and that you will succeed in what Pepik wants so much, in accompanying him when he plays the violin or the viola. Please, do him that favor. I know that it would mean a lot to him, and it would be beautiful. And when you can play well together, play me the aria from Martha: "My rose, you bloom alone there on the hillside," and then: "Sleep my little prince" by Mozart, and then your father's favourite largo: " Under your window" by Chopin. You will play it for me, won't you? I shall always be listening to you.

Just one more thing: Choose your friends carefully. Among other things one is also very much determined by the people with whom one associates. Therefore choose very carefully. Be careful in everything and listen to the opinions of others about your girlfriends without being told. I shall never forget your charming letter (today I can tell you) which you once in the evening pinned to my pillow, to apologize when I caught you for the first time at the gate in the company of a girl and a boy. You explained to me at that time why it is necessary to have a gang. Have your gang, little girl, but of good and clean young people. And compete with each other in everything good. Only please don't confuse young people's springtime infatuation with real love. Do you understand me? If you don't, aunt Vera will help you explain what I meant. And so, my only young daughter, little girl Jana, new life, my hope, my future forgiveness, live! Grasp life with both hands! Until my last breath I shall pray for your happiness, my dear child!

I kiss your hair, eyes and mouth, I stroke you and hold you in my arms (I really held you so

little.) I shall always be with you. I am concluding
by copying from memory the poem which your
father composed for you in jail in 1940 . . .

*There followed a poem written by her husband about the birth of
their daughter — since lost — and a reading list.*

LETTER 24
MY EARTHLY MISSION IS ALREADY
FULFILLED
Vivian Rosewarne to his mother
1940

In May 1940 twenty-three-year-old RAF Flying Officer Vivian Rosewarne was killed during the Battle of Dunkirk when the Wellington bomber he was co-piloting was shot down above Belgium. Shortly after Rosewarne's death, his commander, Group Captain Claude Hilton Keith, discovered an unsealed letter amongst his belongings, to be forwarded to his mother in the event of his death. Such was its impact on his mother and those to whom she showed it, that the next month she gave permission for it to be published anonymously in The Times *to wide acclaim. In fact, the letter was so popular that it was soon published in book form; 500,000 copies were sold that year alone.*

THE LETTER

Dearest Mother:

Though I feel no premonition at all, events are moving rapidly and I have instructed that this letter be forwarded to you should I fail to return from one of the raids that we shall shortly be called upon to undertake. You must hope on for a month, but at the end of that time you must accept the fact that I have handed my task over to the extremely capable hands of my comrades of the Royal Air Force, as so many splendid fellows have already done.

First, it will comfort you to know that my role in this war has been of the greatest importance. Our patrols far out over the North Sea have helped to keep the trade routes clear for our convoys and supply ships, and on one occasion our information was instrumental in saving the lives of the men in a crippled lighthouse relief ship. Though it will be difficult for you, you will disappoint me if you do not at least try to accept the facts dispassionately, for I shall have done my duty to the utmost of my ability. No man can do more, and no one calling himself a man could do less.

I have always admired your amazing courage in the face of continual setbacks; in the way you have given me as good an education and background as anyone in the country: and always kept up appearances without ever losing faith in the future. My death would not mean that your struggle has been in vain. Far from it. It means that your sacrifice is as great as mine. Those who serve England must expect nothing from her; we debase ourselves if we regard our country as merely a place in which to eat and sleep.

History resounds with illustrious names who have given all; yet their sacrifice has resulted in the British Empire where there is a measure of peace, justice and freedom for all, and where a higher standard of civilization has evolved, and is still evolving, than anywhere else. But this is not only concerning our own land. Today we are faced with the greatest organized challenge to Christianity and civilization that the world has ever seen, and I count myself lucky and honoured to be the right age and fully trained to throw my full weight into the scale. For this I have to thank you. Yet there is more work for you to do. The home front will still have to stand united for years after the war is won. For all that can be said against it, I still maintain that this war is a very good thing: every individual is having the chance to give and dare all for his principle like the martyrs of old. However long the time may be, one thing can never be altered – I shall have lived and died an Englishman. Nothing else matters one jot nor can anything ever change it.

You must not grieve for me, for if you really believe in religion and all that it entails that would be hypocrisy. I have no fear of death; only a queer elation . . . I would have it no other way. The universe is so vast and so ageless that the life of one man can only be justified by the measure of his sacrifice. We are sent to this world to acquire a personality and a character to take with us that can never be taken from us. Those who just eat and sleep, prosper and procreate, are no better than animals if all their lives they are at peace.

I firmly believe that evil things are sent into the world to try us; they are sent deliberately by our Creator to test our mettle because He knows what is good for us. The Bible is full of cases where the easy way out has been discarded for moral principles.

I count myself fortunate in that I have seen the whole country and known men of every calling. But with the final test of war I consider my character fully developed. Thus at my early age my earthly mission is already fulfilled and I am prepared to die with just one regret: that I could not devote myself to making your declining years more happy by being with you; but you will live in peace and freedom and I shall have directly contributed to that, so here again my life will not have been in vain.

Your loving son

LETTER 25
YOUR LOVING DAUGHTER
Louisa May Alcott to Abby May Alcott
13 December 1875

On Christmas Day, 1854, fourteen years prior to publication of the first volume of Little Women *– the semi-autobiographical novel for which she would ultimately become known the world over – twenty-two-year-old Louisa May Alcott gave her mother this letter along with a copy of* Flower Fables, *a collection of fairy tales written five years earlier for her friend, Ellen Emerson. Ellen's father, Ralph Waldo Emerson, was a leader in the transcendentalism movement, as was Louisa's father, Amos, a determined man who in the 1840s founded a commune in which his family would live for a short time, and who personally delivered much of his children's education. Despite being dominated by her father, Louisa's strongest bond was with her mother, also a writer, who on the occasion of Louisa's tenth birthday gave her a pencil case along with a note which read, in part, 'Dear Daughter . . . I give you the pencil-case I promised, for I have observed that you are fond of writing, and wish to encourage the habit.'*

THE LETTER

20 Pinckney Street,
Boston,
Dec. 25, 1854

Dear Mother, – Into your Christmas stocking I have put my "first born," knowing that you will accept it with all its faults (for grandmothers are always kind), and look upon it merely as an earnest of what I may yet do; for, with so much to cheer me on, I hope to pass in time from fairies and fables to men and realities.

Whatever beauty or poetry is to be found in my little book is owing to your interest in and encouragement of all my efforts from the first to the last; and if ever I do anything to be proud of, my greatest happiness will be that I can thank you for that, as I may do for all the good there is in me; and I shall be content to write if it gives you pleasure.

Jo is fussing about;
My lamp is going out.

To dear mother, with many kind wishes for a Happy New Year and merry Christmas.

I am ever your loving daughter,
Louy

LETTER 26
I AM WRITING TO YOU FOR THE FIRST
TIME AFTER MY DEATH SENTENCE
Baya Hocine to her mother

Baya Mamadi was born in 1940 in the Casbah of Algiers, only to be orphaned at the age of five and homed with another family. Ten years later, she joined the National Liberation Front, and at sixteen she fought in the Battle of Algiers in an effort to defeat her people's French colonisers. Shortly before Christmas in 1957, this seventeen-year-old freedom fighter, now named Baya Hocine, was arrested and sentenced to death by the French. She informed her mother with the following letter. Hocine's conviction was eventually overturned due to her young age, and in 1962 she was released. She became a journalist and, in 1979, a member of parliament in Algeria where she continued to fight for those in need.

THE LETTER

Mother darling,

I am writing to you for the first time after my
death sentence. My sisters and I received the
sentence with calm and dignity. I hope you will
have the same attitude. I know your courage and I
trust you; I am confident that you will adopt the
right attitude. I have immediately asked for an
appeal; you know now that I will sit for another
trial.

The lawyer saw me yesterday after she met you
during the trial. She was shocked at the sentence
that was pronounced against me. In any case, she
promised to come and see you.

I am well and have everything. You can come
and visit me on Thursday.

I am close to you, aren't I?

I leave you now so that I can make an inventory
of my clothes because our clothes have been
changed to prison clothes.

Kiss the children, Hadjila, my aunt.

My best to the neighbors.

I kiss you tenderly.

Baya

LETTER 27
I LOVE HER MORE THAN ANYTHING
Martha Gellhorn to Lucy Moorehead
1970

Martha Gellhorn was born in St Louis, Missouri, in 1908, one of three children to suffragist Edna and gynaecologist George Gellhorn. By the time of her death in 1998, she had gained a solid reputation as one of the greatest war correspondents in modern history, best known for her reporting during the Spanish Civil War and World War II. In 1970, aged sixty-two, she moved to Knightsbridge where she would stay for the rest of her life. This was also the year that her beloved mother, Edna – once a leading activist and similarly driven – would pass away, aged ninety-one. It was at her ailing mother's side, as she awaited the inevitable, that Martha wrote to her friend, Lucy Moorehead.

THE LETTER

Lucy dear,

Here I am by my mother's death bed, waiting with
her, day after day, for her escape. Her face never
looked tormented in life, and now it looks as if
exhaustion had become pain. She is thin as Belsen,
bones and skin. I can't stop crying when I am with
her – and the rest of the time I have a sensation of
operating in somebody else's dream, not real.
Nothing makes sense or is bearable. I think of you,
10 days beside Alan's bedside while he was in a
coma. If you live long enough you will learn as
much as you can endure. But I always think of the
concentration camps in order to give myself a good
long view on whatever strains I live through. Only
this anguish is for her – when awake, though her
eyes are closed & she is too weak to make words –
I know she knows, and thinks with despair, will I
never be allowed to depart.

I love her more than anything in the world &
always have, my one unfailing love, and now I long
for her to die, to be permitted not to stay where
nothing is left except this overpowering weariness.

I will stay with her as long as she breathes.
Maybe she knows my arms are around her & that I
kiss her hands and maybe feels less lonely. I've seen
so much death but it was all quick. Quick is lucky.
There is no God and no justice. This superb human
being should not have to struggle day after endless
day to leave. Her only passionate act of free will
was to refuse food – the fool nurses push a few
spoonsful of milk down her throat, three times a
day, but I know she is doing the only thing left for
her to stop it all.

Oh Lucy – does one come back into life, after
this, with any slight ability for laughter?

love

Martha

THE LOSS OF YOU LINGERS

Karin Cook to Joan Cook Carpenter

1999

In 1989, fifty-two-year-old Long Island resident Joan Cook Carpenter died from breast cancer, a disease she had chosen to keep from her family and friends until her final days in an effort to minimise the suffering of those she loved. In 1999, a decade after Joan's death, her twenty-nine-year-old daughter, Karin Cook, wrote her this letter. She also wrote an award-winning novel partly inspired by the experience, titled What Girls Learn.

THE LETTER

Dear Mom,
What time was I born?
When did I walk?
What was my first word?

My body has begun to look like yours. Suddenly I
can see you in me. I have so many questions. I look
for answers in the air. Listen for your voice.
Anticipate. Find meaning in the example of your
life. I imagine what you might have said or done.
Sometimes I hear answers in the echo of your
absence. The notion of mentor is always a little
empty for me. Holding out for the hope of you.
My identity has taken shape in spite of that
absence. There are women I go to for advice. But
advice comes from the outside. Knowing, from
within. There is so much I don't know.

What were your secrets?
What was your greatest source of strength?
When did you know you were dying?

I wish I had paid closer attention. The things that
really matter you gave me early on—a way of being
and loving and imagining. It's the stuff of daily life

that is often more challenging. I step unsure into a world of rules and etiquette, not knowing what is expected in many situations. I am lacking a certain kind of confidence. Decisions and departures are difficult. As are dinner parties. Celebrations and ceremony. Any kind of change. Small things become symbolic. Every object matters—that moth-eaten sweater, those photos. Suddenly I care about your silverware. My memory is an album of missed opportunities. The loss of you lingers.

Did you like yourself?
Who was your greatest love?
What did you fear most?

In the weeks before your death, I knew to ask questions. At nineteen, I needed to hear your hopes for me. On your deathbed, you said that you understood my love for women, just as you suggested you would have fought against it. In your absence, I have had to imagine your acceptance.

There are choices I have made that would not have been yours. Somehow that knowledge is harder for me than if I had you to fight with. My motions lack forcefulness. I back into decisions rather than forge ahead. This hesitancy leaves me wondering:

Did you ever doubt me?
Would you have accepted me?
What did you wish for me?

I know that my political choices threatened you. Your
way was to keep things looking good on the
outside, deny certain feelings, erase unpleasant
actions. Since your death, I have exposed many of
the things that you would have liked to keep hidden.
I can no longer hold the family secrets for you.

I search for information about your life. Each
scrapbook, letter, anecdote I come across is crucial
to my desire to understand you and the choices
you made. I have learned about affairs, abuse, all
things you would not have wanted me to know. Yet
they explain the missing blanks in my memory
bank and round out your humanity.

Who did you dream you would be?
Did you ever live alone?
Why did you divorce?
Did you believe in God?

One thing you said haunts me still. When I asked
about motherhood, you said that children don't need
as much as you gave. "Eighty percent is probably
plenty." I was shocked by your words. Did you regret

having given so much of yourself? Now, those words seem like a gift. A way of offering me a model of motherhood, beyond even your own example.

Becoming a mother is something I think about a great deal, almost to the point of preoccupation. I have heard it said that constant dreaming about birth often signals a desire to birth one's self, to come into one's own. My process of grieving the loss of you has been as much about birthing myself as letting you go.

What were your last thoughts?
Were you proud?
Were you at peace?
What is it like to die?

How frightened you must have been shouldering so much of your illness alone. The level of your own isolation is a mystery to me. In my life, I try hard to reach out, to let others in. I fear loss more than anything. I turn on my computer. Make things up. I tell the truth. My daily work is toward connection. All these questions move me to search, less and less for your answers and increasingly for my own.

Love,
Karin

LETTER 29
DEAR DAUGHTERS
Patton Halliday Quinn to Edith Quinn
2015

Patton Halliday Quinn was born in Austin, Texas, and in 2014 gave birth to her daughter, Edith. It was during this pregnancy that Patton wrote a letter to her unborn daughter, filled with advice for Edith to follow in the event of her mother's death. Then, in 2015, with Edith on the scene, Patton had a change of heart.

THE LETTER

Dear Edith,

When you were still in my belly, just after I found
out that you were a girl, in the middle of my preg-
nant-lady-insomnia nights, I wrote you this letter.
I'd take you to New York City for your thirteenth
birthday, and I'd hand you this letter over ice cream
sundaes at Serendipity. I began to worry, though,
What if something happens to me? I wrote and
printed the letter; I tucked it in a place where
you'd be sure to find it. But, I thought, What about
all of the daughters of mothers like mine, who, for
some reason or another, can't, don't, or won't tell
them all the things that they need to know?
    So.

Dear Daughters,

This is *The Talk* that I wished my mother had given
to me. I want you to know so many things and I
don't know what order to put them in, so, I'll
begin in the middle. It's totally okay to have sex
with as many people as you want: boys and girls,
strangers and friends. Never let people shame you
about wanting to experience the fullness of your
humanity. When you do feel guilt or shame about
being human, because there are times that you

will, that's normal too. As much as you can, as often as you can, try to give yourself a break from self-criticism. If you don't want to have sex with someone, that's okay too; just firmly tell them, No! You will eventually find, however, that some men will try to convince you that they won't know that you truly love them unless you have sex with them. Don't buy what they are selling, for it is complete and utter bullshit. BUT, if you do fall for it (like I did), be kind and gentle to yourself when later you realize that you were duped. You aren't the first, and you certainly won't be the last.

Be careful. I can't stress this enough. Get pap smears regularly; get STD tests regularly; get the HPV vaccine. Get on birth control and ask him to wear a condom. If he doesn't put a condom on – which there will be a time when he doesn't and you will let him get away with it – make sure that he pulls out. If, by mistake, you get pregnant (like I did), know that it's okay to have an abortion. Of course, you don't want that to be your only form of birth control, OF COURSE. But. Most women I know have had at least one. Just know having an abortion does come with emotional consequences. Some women feel regret immediately. Some women feel regret later, in their late-thirties, when they realize that their window is closing. I felt relief immediately; however, not a year goes by that I don't say to myself, "If I had her, she'd be twelve now." Also, if you have an abortion, talk about it. The secretive nature of abortions is what contributes to the stigmatized nature of abortions.

If you are gay, that's fine. If you are transgender, that's fine. If you are straight, that's fine. Just be you, but if you want to try to be someone else for a while, that's totally understandable too.

There are issues specific to promiscuous sex and dating. There were some boys I could have sex with and be friends with and not get obsessive about, and there were others who I'd fall in love with, boys who would never love me back. I'd get all loopy in the head. I'd wait, impatiently, for a phone call or text that would never come. Unfortunately, that's part of it. Unrequited love is the most crushing feeling you will ever feel.

There is a separate set of issues you will discover in monogamous relationships. Avoid the following: wanting to look good for him, seeking approval from him, or relying on him to boost yourself confidence. You will make this mistake, probably more than once, and that's okay. Don't cheat or lie, to him or to yourself. If you do – admit it, apologize, journal and reflect about why you did it, and then begin the painful process of forgiving yourself.

Remember that love is always painful and messy and hard, but that it's always healing and messy and good too.

There will be times that you are so hurt, times when you didn't feel it was possible to be in so much pain. Edith, when I was pregnant with you, your Dad left me to gamble and pursue a meth addiction and the heartbreak I felt was so deep and so painful that I swore off love forever. Or so I thought. Don't be surprised to learn that, when and if you think you've successfully shut your heart off for good, the universe may have other plans. I worked every day, for many days in a row, to forgive your father. One day I finally concluded that love couldn't be as painful as loneliness, and so I opened up my heart again. I found that the pain actually could go deeper, but that my chasmic threshold for sadness only meant that I get to feel love that much more.

Daughters, there will come a time when you feel alone in the universe, but I'm here to tell you that you are not. Because all of the mothers are right here behind you. We are propping you up; we are holding your hand; we are making sure that you are still breathing. We love you, we support you, we forgive you, we understand you, and it's all going to be okay.

This letter started as a letter to you, dear Edith. Then became a letter to all of the daughters. It's also a letter to all of the moms and all the not-moms. It's really, I see now, probably, mostly a letter to me.

I love you more than the most,
Mom

LETTER 30
MOM, LISTEN
Wallace Stegner to Hilda Stegner
1989

In 1909, in Lake Mills, Iowa, Hilda and George Stegner
welcomed a son into the world who would go on to
become one of the most revered writers of all time.
During a career that lasted more than half a century,
Wallace Stegner won practically every award available
to an author, including, in 1972, the Pulitzer Prize for
Fiction. He was also a committed environmentalist. His
relationship with his parents was one of mixed
emotions: his father, a restless gambler, constantly
dragged the family from town to town; his mother,
who he loved dearly, simply yearned to settle down.
She passed away in 1933, four years after Wallace's
brother died of pneumonia. Fifty-five years later,
Stegner wrote his mother a letter.

THE LETTER

Mom, listen.

In three months I will be eighty years old, thirty years older than you were when you died, twenty years older than my father was when he died, fifty-seven years older than my brother was when he died. I got the genes and the luck. The rest of you have been gone a long time.

Except when I have to tie my shoelaces, I don't feel eighty years old. I, the sickly child, have outlasted you all. But if I don't feel decrepit, neither do I feel wise or confident. Age and experience have not made me a Nestor qualified to tell others about how to live their lives. I feel more like Theodore Dreiser, who confessed that he would depart from life more bewildered than he had arrived in it. Instead of being embittered, or stoical, or calm, or resigned, or any of the standard things that a long life might have made me, I confess that I am often simply lost, as much in need of comfort, understanding, forgiveness, uncritical love – the things you used to give me – as I ever was at five, or ten, or fifteen.

Fifty-five years ago, sitting up with you after midnight while the nurse rested, I watched you take your last breath. A few minutes before you

died you half raised your head and said, "Which
. . . way?" I understood that: you were at a dark,
unmarked crossing. Then a minute later you said,
"You're a good . . . boy . . . Wallace," and died.

My name was the last word you spoke, your
faith in me and love for me were your last
thoughts. I could bear them no better than I could
bear your death, and I went blindly out into the
November darkness and walked for hours with my
mind clenched like a fist.

I knew how far from true your last words were.
There had been plenty of times when I had not
been a good boy or a thoughtful one. I knew you
could no longer see my face, that you spoke from a
clouded, drugged dream, that I had already faded
to a memory that you clung to even while you
waned from life. I knew that it was love speaking,
not you, that you had already gone, that your love
lasted longer than you yourself did. And I had
some dim awareness that as you went away you
laid on me an immense and unavoidable obligation.
I would never get over trying, however badly or
sadly or confusedly, to be what you thought I was.

Obviously you did not die. Death is a convention, a certification to the end of pain, something
for the vital-statistics book, not binding upon
anyone but the keepers of graveyard records. For as

I sit here at the desk, trying to tell you something fifty-five years too late, I have a clear mental image of your pursed lips and your crinkling eyes, and I know that nothing I can say will persuade you that I was ever less than you thought me. Your kind of love, once given, is never lost. You are alive and luminous in my head. Except when I fail to listen, you will speak through me when I face some crisis of feeling or sympathy or consideration for others. You are a curb on my natural impatience and competitiveness and arrogance. When I have been less than myself, you make me ashamed even as you forgive me. You're a good . . . boy . . . Wallace.

In the more than fifty years that I have been writing books and stories, I have tried several times to do you justice, and have never been satisfied with what I did. The character who represents you in *The Big Rock Candy Mountain* and *Recapitulation*, two novels of a semiautobiographical kind, is a sort of passive victim. I am afraid I let your selfish and violent husband, my father, steal the scene from you and push you into the background in the novels as he did in life. Somehow I should have been able to say how strong and resilient you were, what a patient and abiding and bonding force, the softness that proved in the long run stronger than what it seemed to yield to.

But you must understand that you are the hardest sort of human character to make credible on paper. We are skeptical of kindness so unfailing, sympathy so instant and constant, trouble so patiently borne, forgiveness so whole-hearted. Writing about you, I felt always on the edge of the unbelievable, as if I were writing a saint's life, or the legend of some Patient Griselda. I felt that I should warp you a little, give you some human failing or selfish motive; for saintly qualities, besides looking sentimental on the page, are a rebuke to those – and they are most of us – who have failed at them. What is more, saintly and long-suffering women tend to infuriate the current partisans of women's liberation, who look upon them as a masculine invention, the too submissive and too much praised victims of male dominance.

Well, you were seldom aggressive, not by the time I knew you, and you were an authentic victim. How truly submissive, that is another matter. Some, I suppose, are born unselfish, some achieve unselfishness, and some have unselfishness thrust upon them. You used to tell me that you were born with a redheaded temper, and had to learn to control it. I think you were also born with a normal complement of dreams and hopes and desires and a great capacity for intellectual and cultural growth, and had to learn to suppress them.

Your life gave you plenty of practice in both controlling and suppressing. You were robbed of your childhood, and as a young, inexperienced woman you made a fatal love choice. But you blamed no one but yourself. You lay in the bed you had made, partly because, as a woman, and without much education, you had few options, and partly because your morality counseled responsibility for what you did, but mostly because love told you your highest obligation was to look after your two boys and the feckless husband who needed you more even than they did. Your reward, all too often, was to be taken for granted.

Just now, thinking about you, I got out *The Big Rock Candy Mountain* and found the passage in which I wrote of your death. I couldn't bear to read it. It broke me down in tears to read the words that I wrote in tears nearly a half century ago. You are at once a lasting presence and an unhealed wound.

I was twenty-four, still a schoolboy, when you died, but I have lived with you more than three times twenty-four years. Self-obsessed, sports crazy or book crazy or girl crazy or otherwise preoccupied, I never got around to telling you during your lifetime how much you meant. Except in those moments when your life bore down on you with particular weight, as when my brother, Cece, died and you turned to me because you had no one else, I don't suppose I realized how much you meant. Now I feel mainly regret, regret that I took you for granted as the others did, regret that you were dead by the time my life began to expand, so that I was unable to take you along and compensate you a little for your first fifty years. Cinderella should end happily, released from the unwholesome house of her servitude.

One of my friends in that later life that you did not live to share was the Irish writer Frank O'Connor, who was born Michael O'Donovan in a shabby cottage in Cork. His father was a drunk; his mother, he firmly believed, was a saint. He put her into many of his short stories, and he wrote her a book of tribute called *An Only Child.* Though he was not much of a Catholic, he expected to meet her in heaven, garbed in glory. From what he told me, she was much like you: she was incomparably herself, and yet she always thought of herself last. I can't believe that he is with her now in heaven, though I wish I could. I can't believe either that eventually, pretty soon in fact, I will meet you there. But what a reunion that would be! It would be worth conversion to assure it – the four of us enjoying whatever it is that immortals enjoy, and enjoying it together. I admired Frank O'Connor for his great gifts; but I loved Michael O'Donovan for the way he felt about his mother, and envied him for the chance he got, as a mature man, to show it. If the man-dominated world, with all its injustices, now and then produces women like his mother and mine, it can't be all bad.

I began this rumination in a dark mood, remembering the anniversary of your death. Already you have cheered me up. I have said that you didn't die, and you didn't. I can still hear you being cheerful on the slightest provocation, or no provocation at all, singing as you work and shedding your cheerfulness on others. So let us remember your life, such a life as many women of your generation shared to some extent, though not always with your special trials and rarely with your stoicism and grace.

*

I have heard enough about your childhood and youth to know how life went on that Iowa farm and in the town where everybody spoke Norwegian, read Norwegian, did business in Norwegian, heard Norwegian in church. The family

Bible that somehow descended to me is in Norwegian, and in Gothic type at that. Next to it on my shelf is the preposterous five-pound book that they gave you on your fifth birthday: *Sandheden i Kristus*, Truths in Christ, a compendium of instructions and meditations geared to the religious year. You would have had to be as old as I am, and as rigid a Lutheran as your father, to tolerate five minutes of it.

Though your father was born in this country, you did not learn English until you started school. You learned it eagerly. Some of our mutual relatives, after five generations in the United States, still speak with an accent, but you never did. You loved reading, and you sang all the time: you knew the words to a thousand songs. When I was in college I was astonished to discover that some songs I had heard you sing as you worked around the house were lyrics from Tennyson's *The Princess*. Maybe you got the words from *McGuffey's Reader*. Where you got the tunes, God knows. You always made the most of what little was offered you, and you kept hold of it.

School was your happy time, with friends, games, parties, the delight of learning. You had it for only six years. When you were twelve, your mother died of tuberculosis and you became an instant adult: housekeeper to your father, mother to your two younger brothers and sister, farmhand when not otherwise employed. All through the years when you should have had the chance to be girlish, even frivolous, you had responsibilities that would have broken down most adults.

Many farm wives had a "hired girl." You did not. You were It, you did it all. At twelve, thirteen, fourteen, you made beds, cleaned, cooked, sewed, mended, for a family of five. You baked the bread, biscuits, cakes, pies, in a cranky coal range. You made the *lefse* and *fattigmand* and prepared the *lutefisk* without which a Norwegian Christmas is not Christmas. You washed all the clothes, and I don't mean you put lightly soiled clothes into a washing machine. I mean you boiled and scrubbed dirty farm clothes with only the copper boiler, tin tub, brass washboard, harsh soap, and hand wringer of the 1890s – one long backbreaking day every week.

At harvest time you often worked in the field most of the morning and then came in to cook dinner for the crew. You were over a hot stove in a suffocating kitchen for hours at a time, canning peas, beans, corn, tomatoes, putting up cucumber and watermelon pickles or piccalilli. When a hog was slaughtered, you swallowed your nausea and caught the blood for the blood pudding your father relished. You pickled pigs' feet and made head-cheese. You fried and put down in crocks of their own lard the sausage patties that would last all winter. Morning and evening you helped with the milking. You skimmed the cream and churned the butter in the dasher churn, you hung cheesecloth bags of curd on the clothesline to drip and become cottage cheese. Maybe you got a little help from your brothers and sister, especially as they got older; but they were in school all day, and whined about having homework at night.

I am sure there were times when you bitterly resented your bond-servant life, when you thumped your lazy and evasive brothers, or sent hot glances at your father where he sat reading *Scandinaven* in the parlor, totally unaware of you as you staggered in with a scuttle of coal and set it down loudly by the heater, and opened the heater door and lifted the scuttle and fed the fire and set the scuttle down again and slammed the heater door with a bang. Those were the years when you had unselfishness thrust upon you; you had not yet got through the difficult process of achieving it.

But however you might rebel, there was no shedding your siblings. They were your responsibility and there was no one to relieve you of them. They called you Sis. All your life people called you

Sis, because that was what you were, or what you became – big sister, helpful sister, the one upon whom everyone depended, the one they all came to for everything from help with homework to a sliver under the fingernail.

Six years of that, at the end of which your father announced that he was going to marry a school friend of yours, a girl barely older than yourself. I wonder if it was outrage that drove you from his house, or if your anger was not lightened by the perception that here at last was freedom and opportunity. You were eighteen, a tall, strong, direct-eyed girl with a pile of gorgeous red hair. In the tintypes of the time you look determined. You do not yet have the sad mouth your last photographs show. Maybe the world then seemed all before you, your imprisonment over.

But nobody had prepared you for opportunity and freedom. Nobody had taught you to dream big. You couldn't have imagined going to Chicago or New York and winning your way, you could never have dreamed of becoming an actress or the editor of a women's magazine. They had only taught you, and most of that you had learned on your own, to keep house and to look after others. You were very good at both. So when you were displaced as your father's housekeeper, you could think of nothing better to do with your freedom than to go to North Dakota and keep house for a bachelor uncle.

There you met something else they had not prepared you for, a man unlike any you had ever seen, a husky, laughing, reckless, irreverent, story-telling charmer, a ballplayer, a fancy skater, a trapshooting champion, a pursuer of the main chance, a true believer in the American dream of something for, nothing, a rolling stone who confidently expected to be eventually covered with moss. He was marking time between get-rich-quick schemes by running a "blind pig" – an illegal saloon. He offended every piety your father stood for. Perhaps that was why you married him, against loud protests from home. Perhaps your father was as much to blame as anyone for the mistake you made.

You had a stillborn child. Later you had a living one, my brother, Cecil. Later still, on a peacemaking visit back to Iowa, you had me. Then, as you told me once, you discovered how not to have any more, and didn't. You had enough to be responsible for with two.

To run through your life would be lugubrious if it were not you we were talking about. You made it something else by your total competence, your cheerfulness under most uncheerful conditions, your resilience after every defeat. "Better luck next time!" I have heard you say as we fled from some disaster, and after a minute, with your special mixture of endurance, hope, and irony, "Well, if it didn't kill us, I guess it must have been good for us."

Dakota I don't remember. My memories begin in the woods of Washington, where we lived in a tent and ran a lunchroom in the logging town of Redmond. By getting scarlet fever, I had balked father's dream of going to Alaska and digging up baseball sized nuggets. Then there was a bad time. You left my father, or he you; nobody ever told me. But Cece and I found ourselves in a Seattle orphans' home, put there while you worked the Bon Marche. In 1913 you didn't have a chance as a husbandless woman with two children. When you found how miserable we were in that home, you took us out and brought us back to the only safety available, your father's house in Iowa.

I can imagine what that cost you in humiliation. I can imagine the letters that must have passed between you and my father. I can imagine his promises, your concessions. At any rate, in June 14 we were on our way to join him in the valley of the Whitemud, or Frenchman, River in Saskatchewan. Perhaps it sounded romantic and adventurous to you, perhaps you let yourself listen to his come-all-ye enthusiasm, perhaps you thought that on a real frontier he might be happy and do well. Very likely you hoped that in a raw village five hundred miles from anywhere we could make a new start and be a family, something for which you had both a yearning and a gift. If you went in resignation, this time your resignation was not forced on you. It was a choice. By 1914, at the age of thirty-one, you had finally achieved unselfishness.

Saskatchewan is the richest page in my memory, for that was where I first began to understand some things, and that was where, for a half dozen years, we had what you had always wanted: a house of our own, a united family, and a living, however hard.

I remember good days for the shared pleasure we took in them – family expeditions to pick berries in the Cypress Hills, when we picnicked on the edge of Chimney Coulee and watched great fleets of clouds sail eastward over the prairie. Raising a sandwich to your mouth, you exclaimed, "Oh! Smell your hands!" and we did, inhaling the fragrance of the saskatoons, gooseberries, choke-cherries, pin cherries, and highbush cranberries we had been working in. I remember that on our way home from one of those expeditions the democrat wagon tipped over on a steep hillside and spilled us and our overflowing pans and pails of berries out onto the grass. You took one quick look to see if anyone was hurt, and then began to laugh, pointing to the embarrassed and bewildered team standing among the twisted tugs. We sat in the sudden grass and laughed ourselves silly before we got up and scraped together the spilled berries and straightened out the buggy and relieved the team and drove home. Singing, naturally. You never lost an opportunity to sing. You sang, too, among the rich smells in the kitchen as you made those wild berries into pies and jams and sauces and jellies and put a lot of them up in jars and glasses to be stored on the cellar shelves.

Do you remember a day on the homestead when Pa came back from Chinook with a big watermelon, and we cooled it as well as we could in the reservoir and then sat down in the shade of the shack and ate it all? How simple and memorable a good day can be when expectation is low! You made us save the rinds for pickles. Your training had been thorough, you never wasted anything. One of our neighbors, years later, wrote me about how amazed he was to see you, after you had peeled a lot of apples and made pies of them, boil up the peelings and turn them into jelly.

I think you loved that little burg in spite of its limitations.

You loved having neighbors, visiting with neighbors, helping neighbors. When it was our turn to host the monthly Sunday school party, you had more fun than the kids, playing crocinole or beanbag like the child you had never been allowed to be. You loved the times when the river froze without wind or snow, and the whole channel was clean, skatable ice, and the town gathered around big night fires, and skaters in red mackinaws and bright scarfs moved like Brueghel figures across the light, and firelight glinted off eyeballs and teeth, and the breath of the community went up in white plumes.

You loved having your children in a steady school, and doing well in it. You read all the books you could lay hands on. When your North Dakota uncle died and left you a thousand dollars you didn't let my father take it, though I am sure he would have found a use for it. Instead, you bought a Sears, Roebuck piano and you set my brother and me to learn to play it under the instruction of the French doctor's wife. Alas, we disappointed you, resisted practice, dawdled and fooled around. Eventually you gave up. But you could no more let that piano sit there unused than you could throw perfectly good apple peelings out to the pig. You learned to play it yourself, painstakingly working things out chord by chord from the sheet music of popular songs. How hungry you were! How you would have responded to the opportunities ignored by so many who have them!

Many good days. Also, increasingly, bad ones. Hard times.

While you lived your way deeper into the remote and limited place where my father's enthusiasms had brought you, he felt more and more trapped in what he called "this dirty little dung-heeled sagebrush town." On the homestead where we spent our summers, he had made one good and one average crop out of five. One summer he grew hundreds of bushels of potatoes on rented bottomland near town and stored them in the basement of the hotel, waiting for the right price, and the hotel burned down. That winter he supported us by playing poker. By the summer of 1920 he was raging to get out, do something, find some way of making a real living.

Eventually he got his way, and we abandoned what little you had been able to get together as a life. During the next fourteen years you lived in much greater comfort, and you saw a lot of the western United States. You continued to make a home for your boys and your husband, but it was a cheerless home for you. We lived in a dozen towns and cities, three dozen neighborhoods, half a hundred houses. My brother and I kept some continuity through school and the friends we made there, but your continuity was cut every few months; you lost friends and never saw them again, or got the chance to make new ones, or have a kitchen where women could drop in and have a cup of coffee and a chat. Too much of your time, in Great Falls, Salt Lake, Reno, Los Angeles, Long Beach, you were alone.

You believed in all the beauties and strengths and human associations of place; my father believed only in movement. You believed in a life of giving, he in a life of getting. When Cecil died at the age of twenty-three, you did not have a single woman friend to whom you could talk, not a single family of neighbors or friends to help you bear the loss of half your loving life.

You're a good . . . boy . . . Wallace. That shames me. You had little in your life to judge goodness by. I was not as dense or as selfish as my father, and I got more credit than I deserved. But I was not intelligent enough to comprehend the kind of example you had been setting me, until it was too late to do anything but hold your hand while you died. And here I am, nearly eighty years old, too old to be capable of any significant improvement but not too old for regret.

"All you can do is try," you used to tell me when I was scared of undertaking something. You got me to undertake many things I would not have dared undertake without your encouragement. You also taught me how to take defeat when it came, and it was bound to now and then. You taught me that if it hadn't killed me it was probably good for me.

I can hear you laugh while you say it. Any minute now I will hear you singing.

PERMISSION CREDITS

LETTER 1 Reprinted by kind permission of Melissa Rivers.

LETTER 2 Reprinted by permission of SLL/Sterling Lord Literistic, Inc. Copyright © 1981 by Linda Gray Sexton and Loring Conant, Jr.

LETTER 3 Reprinted with kind permission of Danny DeVito and Kirk Douglas. With thanks to CAA.

LETTER 4 Reprinted by kind permission of Caitlin Moran.

LETTER 5 Copyright © 1936 by White Literary, LLC. Reprinted by permission of ICM Partners.

LETTER 7 Reprinted by kind permission of Claude Bernard and in memory of his sister Dorothy Jackson.

LETTER 8 With thanks to B.D. Hyman.

LETTER 9 Reprinted by kind permission of Renée C. Neblett.

LETTER 11 Reprinted with the kind permission of Hannah Woodhead.

LETTER 12 The Society of Authors, on behalf of the Bernard Shaw Estate.

LETTER 14 Edna St. Vincent Millay, letter of June 15, 1921 from *Letters of Edna St. Vincent Millay*, edited by Allan Ross Macdougall. Copyright © 1952 and renewed copyright © 1980 by Norma Millay Ellis / Reprinted with the permission of The Permissions Company, LLC on behalf of Holly Peppe, Literary Executor, The Edna St. Vincent Millay Society, www.millay.org.

LETTER 15 Reprinted by arrangement with The Heirs to the Estate of Martin Luther King Jr., c/o Writers House as agent for the proprietor New York, NY / Copyright © 1951 Dr. Martin Luther King, Jr. copyright © renewed 1979 Coretta Scott King.

LETTER 16 From *Letters Home* by Sylvia Plath, reprinted by permission of Faber & Faber Ltd.

LETTER 17 Reproduced with permission of Curtis Brown, London, on behalf of The Master, Fellows and Scholars of Churchill College, Cambridge © The Master, Fellows and Scholars of Churchill College, Cambridge / Reproduced with permission of Curtis Brown, London, on behalf of The Estate of Winston S. Churchill. Copyright © The Estate of Winston S. Churchill.

LETTER 18 Reprinted by kind permission of Laura Dern.

LETTER 19 Reprinted by kind permission of Tina Le Blanc

ACKNOWLEDGEMENTS

It requires a dedicated team of incredibly patient people to bring the *Letters of Note* books to life, and this page serves as a heartfelt thank you to every single one of them, beginning with my wife, Karina – not just for kickstarting my obsession with letters all those years ago, but for working with me as Permissions Editor, a vital and complex role. Special mention, also, to my excellent editor at Canongate Books, Hannah Knowles, who has somehow managed to stay focused despite the problems I have continued to throw her way.

Equally sincere thanks to all of the following: the one and only Jamie Byng, whose vision and enthusiasm for this series has proven invaluable; all at Canongate Books, including but not limited to Rafi Romaya, Kate Gibb, Vicki Rutherford and Leila Cruickshank; my dear family at Letters Live: Jamie, Adam Ackland, Benedict Cumberbatch, Aimie Sullivan, Amelia Richards and Nick Allott; my agent, Caroline Michel, and everyone else at Peters, Fraser & Dunlop; the many illustrators who have worked on the beautiful covers in this series; the talented performers who have lent their stunning voices not just to Letters Live, but also to the *Letters of Note* audiobooks; Patti Pirooz; every single archivist and librarian in the world; everyone at Unbound; the team at the Wylie Agency for their assistance and understanding; my foreign publishers for their continued support; and, crucially, my family, for putting up with me during this process.

Finally, and most importantly, thank you to all of the letter writers whose words feature in these books.